HARD STOP

PRAISE FOR *HARD STOP*

"*Hard Stop* by Gina Boedeker is a compelling and insightful read that delves into the crucial practice of introspection and boundary-setting in one's life. It's not just about stopping certain activities; it's a guide to starting to live more intentionally, providing an invitation to readers to reassess their commitments, realign their actions with their values, and make space for growth and contentment. Boedeker's book is a must-read for anyone looking to declutter their life, prioritize their well-being, and embark on a journey of self-improvement. It's a powerful reminder that sometimes, the most productive thing one can do is to take a step back and evaluate the direction in which they are heading."

— Cathy Fyock

"Gina's work is what every driven professional needs to read—it explains how to figure out and pursue your passion without losing yourself and what else is important to you. Her insights and wisdom are helping me determine how to be the best leader and version of myself I want to be."

— Heidi Rhinehart

"As soon as I picked this up, something automatically made sense to me. Seeking balance in your professional and personal life. It's acceptable to need self care or family time while simultaneously doing your job. No one should make you feel as though professional life comes before personal. Your life is yours to live, and you should not compromise for anyone."

— Amanda Dell

"Gina's willingness to open up about her life and share her challenges with work-life balance is both refreshing and inspiring. Her journey from being a big city, hard-charging corporate ladder climber to seeking more equilibrium in her life is one that many of us can relate to. The scales of life can be tricky to balance, and Gina's stories of blending family and work, when to say 'no,' and more importantly, when to say 'yes,' show that it is possible to set boundaries, live intentionally, and succeed professionally and personally. Gina's *Hard Stop* approach is more than a philosophy. Rather, it is a practical and tangible method we all can embrace to achieve greater fulfillment at home, at work, and in our communities."

— Ed Dillon

"It's so important to have real conversations about real-life challenges; that is exactly what Gina and *Hard Stop* address. *Hard Stop* is the opposite of the 'Insta' version of life that we often see. Instead, Gina is vulnerable in her topics and she shares incredibly helpful and useful tactics and tips."

— Brenda Abdilla

"Never in my life has a book so inspired me to pick up a pen and a journal and really *do* the activities inside it—and I have read more than my fair share of self-help and business strategy books! *Hard Stop* is chock-full of practical advice—practical, *not* necessarily easy—on how to determine what you truly want from your life and how to go after it with intentionality. Anyone who has been working, or "adulting" (as my kids and their friends might say), for more than just a couple of years can relate to the examples in this book. I have one piece of advice for anyone who picks up this book. Read the introduction! I know lots of people skip an introduction in order to get "straight to the good stuff" that begins in the first chapter of a book. Trust me, though; if you read Jane's story in the intro, you will see yourself in at least some aspect of her story and better understand how we can all benefit from *Hard Stop*."

— Terri Davis

"*Hard Stop* is the new roadmap for business leaders and entrepreneurs in a post-COVID world who are looking to make sense of balancing work and life. Having known and worked with Gina personally, I witnessed her transition from a demanding leadership role in a Fortune 500 company to reinventing herself as both a successful entrepreneur and wife and mother. What I love most about *Hard Stop* is not spewing buzzwords or selling a magic formula—it's packed with honesty, it focuses on intentional living, and recognizes that life is, well, sometimes hard!

"*Hard Stop* coaches readers to consider how everyday choices we make based on our intentions shape our lives in meaningful ways. It's not about having it all, it's about creating boundaries to protect what is truly important."

— Ryan Blankenship

"Re-centering. That's the continuous impact that *Hard Stop* has had on me during one of the most tumultuous times in my career (because of layoffs, existential crisis, and that thing called #momlife, the struggle was/is real). With *Hard Stop*, Gina gives us a gentle but no-nonsense nudge to become action-oriented in creating meaning and intention in our lives, especially when many things can easily consume us. Her storytelling is relatable, making it easy for readers to say "oh my, me too!" When my path is cluttered and distracted, I re-center with *Hard Stop*, a new addition to my *namaste* routine."

— Lindsey Gervais

"Gina provides information in *Hard Stop* that is based on her personal experiences. Gina provides a personal story that is on topic along with informative insights, an inspirational mindset, and easy steps forward for readers to implement into their own personal situations. Especially helpful are Gina's writings on seeking balance in our career and personal lives where she shares gems of wisdom!"

— Phil Garcia

"*Hard Stop* is like a roadmap for making life more meaningful. It's full of smart ideas on how to figure out what really matters, set clear boundaries, and find time for things that make life awesome. If you're looking to step up your game and live with intention, this book is a game-changer."

— Melissa Janis

"Reading this book transformed my relationship with my calendar! I feel a new sense of agency in creating a customized future for myself and my family—ditching the 24/7 working mom overwhelm for more balance, fulfillment, and joyful experiences. Gina's self-reflections, journaling prompts, and life strategies are brilliant. Get ready for big realizations that lead to meaningful results! *Hard Stop* is lighthearted, fun to read, and full of wise gems—and it will change your life."

— Katie Crouch

HARD STOP

LIVE WITH INTENTION
AND WITHOUT REGRET

GINA BOEDEKER

Publishing support provided by
Ignite Press
55 Shaw Ave. Suite 204
www.IgnitePress.us
Clovis, CA 93612
www.IgnitePress.us

ISBN: 979-8-9903049-0-1
ISBN: 979-8-9903049-1-8 (E-book)

For bulk purchases and for booking, contact:

Gina Boedeker
www.ginaboedeker.com

Library of Congress Control Number: 2024906057

Cover design by Usman Tariq
Edited by Elizabeth Arterberry
Interior design by Jetlaunch

FIRST EDITION

To my parents, Bill and Judy Boedeker, who have always made family their top priority, teaching me about the importance of work-life balance before it was even a "thing."

To Elena and Luiz, who highlight for me every day what is most important in my life, and who motivate me to be the best version of myself I can be (and the best mom to them)!

*And to Otavio, who has brought more fun and adventure to my life than I thought possible. I'm tired sometimes ;) but I **love** the life we have built together.*

I love you all and appreciate you more than you know.

Acknowledgments

Writing a book is a journey that involves the support and contributions of many individuals. I am grateful to those who have played a crucial role in the creation of *Hard Stop.* Their encouragement, expertise, and unwavering support have been invaluable.

To my Editorial Board—Alicia Brady, Angie Carlson, Cathy Fyock, Katie Crouch, and Terri Davis—**thank you!** I invited you to be a part of this process because I think so highly of each of you individually and knew that, as a group, you would make this book better. You're smart, creative, driven women who have always understood the message that I wanted to send in this book. You also are highly opinionated, strong in your convictions, and unafraid to be honest with your feedback. I needed that. You made *Hard Stop* better by being honest with me, and I can't thank you enough for your candor.

I am grateful to Everett O'Keefe and the team at Ignite, especially Elizabeth Arterberry, for their editorial guidance and keen insights that have transformed this manuscript into a polished and cohesive piece of work. Ignite's dedication to excellence is truly commendable.

A little over a year ago, I took an accelerator course with Kait LeDonne because I knew I wanted to share my message about intentionality, but wasn't sure how to write about intentionality on the social channels I use to grow my market research business. It was unclear to me how those messages would work together and how they would be received. She helped me refine my voice, encouraged me on this journey, and helped come up with the *Hard Stop* newsletter that got this process in motion. Kait, thank you so much!

I've been fortunate in my corporate career, and now, as the owner of a business, to work with people who respect my passion about work-life balance. I've always had the opportunity to have leadership teams who appreciated that balance was necessary for me, and I know how fortunate I am for that. Now I have the opportunity to support clients who can appreciate me as a whole person, who has desires outside of work in addition to delivering on their project goals. They recognize you can strive for work-life harmony without sacrificing on quality, and that they trust me and my team with their most important projects means the world to me.

My family is my *"why."* They are the reason I want to schedule my time around my priorities, because making memories with them is what matters most to me in my life. From the moment I was pregnant with my daughter, I knew I'd have to find a way to make my work and life intersect in a way that I could feel successful as a professional *and* as a mom. It's a constant balancing act, but my desire to be as present with all of them as much as possible while building a successful business and making time for my health, happiness, and hobbies is all the motivation I need.

Finally, to the readers who will engage with this book and those who have loyally followed the *Hard Stop* newsletter: Thank *you*. Your curiosity and willingness to explore the concept of intentionality contributes to the larger conversation about its importance in corporate settings, and for that, I am truly thankful.

This book would not have been possible without the collective effort and generosity of all of these individuals. I am deeply appreciative of their contributions, which will help more people get on with living their best lives.

Thank you so much for allowing me to be a part of your journey.

"Regret for things we did can be tempered over time. It is regret for things we have not done that is inconsolable."

— Sidney J. Harris

Note to the Reader:

Dear reader,

As you embark on this journey of intentional living within the pages that follow, it is important that I pause and recognize the vast spectrum of experiences and challenges that shape each of our individual lives. While the intention of this book is to offer practical insights and suggestions for leading a more intentional life, it is essential that I begin by acknowledging the limits inherent in *any* book, written by *one* person, to speak to the wide array of circumstances that could impact a person's ability to implement these suggestions.

As the author, I am acutely aware that my perspective is inherently limited by my own life experiences and the lens through which I view the world. This recognition prompts me to acknowledge the blind spots that may be present in these pages. Areas such as alcohol abuse, drug dependencies, domestic violence, trauma, and countless others, might not be fully realized or sufficiently addressed when I provide practical tips for living more intentionally.

Hard Stop is not a one-size-fits-all solution, nor does it claim to have all the answers. It is an offering, a collection of ideas and practices that may or may not align with your individual circumstances. I encourage you to approach these pages with an open heart and a discerning mind, adapting the content to suit your own needs and seeking professional guidance where necessary. It is my hope that, no matter your circumstances, you may discover nuggets of wisdom, or inspiration, and tools that resonate with you.

May this book serve as a companion as you each embark on your intentionality journey, providing support, encouragement, and perhaps a new perspective. It is my sincere wish that, as you navigate the terrain of intentional living, you find the strength to weave your unique path of purpose and fulfillment.

Respectfully,

Gina

Table of Contents

Introduction

Meet Jane.

Jane works all day as a health care director at a hospital.

This morning, like yesterday morning, the morning before that, and the morning before that— every morning that she can remember, really—she wakes up tired. She had a long night of tossing and turning; the upcoming day's responsibilities were on her mind as she struggled to get just a little bit more much-needed sleep. She quickly showers, gets dressed, quickly brushes through her hair, and slaps on some makeup before running downstairs. She yells at her kids to get up, get moving, and runs through the house getting their things together so they will be on time for the bus, grabbing her bag so she, too, can make it to work on time. En route to her office, she runs through a drive-through coffee shop for the necessary triple shot espresso and a muffin.

At work, she's running on adrenaline, yet tired. It's hard to stay awake. She is in back-to-back meetings all morning, she has a big project deadline coming up, and hasn't had a moment to think about it, much less work on it, given her Zoom and in-person meeting marathons. She grabs some takeout that she wolfs down during a meeting, liberally turning off the camera when she needs to chew, and starts to feel the impact of her restless sleep. So, after lunch, she picks up another coffee and a sweet from the break room to get through the rest of the afternoon.

She spends the afternoon working on her imminent deadline, but has to run out right at 4:30 to get her kids to their music lessons. While out, she grabs her drycleaning and picks up some things she needs for dinner. She preps dinner and, while it's cooking in the oven, she walks around, picking up legos, books, and discarded socks (everywhere!) in the effort of combatting the tidal wave of messiness for one more day. She sits to eat dinner with her family, cleans up all the dishes and puts the kitchen back in order, gets the kids to begrudgingly brush their teeth, get ready for bed, and turn off devices.

By the time she looks at the clock, it's 9:15 and she's fall-down tired, but too wired to sleep, and she hasn't had a moment to herself all day—not to mention time to spend with her partner. So, she pours a glass of wine, logs into Netflix to watch her newest series obsession, and spends some "quality time" with her partner. Before she knows it, she wakes up at midnight, having fallen asleep on the couch while watching her show. She gets up, washes her face, brushes her teeth, and falls down onto her bed, but she's woken up enough now that her mind is racing with thoughts about everything she has to do tomorrow. She tosses and turns, thinks about the upcoming day, and pleads to whatever in the universe is out there listening to *please* just give her a few hours of precious sleep.

Then she does it again the next day.

Jane is in trouble. She's in a cycle that's harming her health and impacting the quality of her life and that of those around her. But here is the kicker. On paper, she has everything she has always wanted. She has a good job, a loving partner, two kids, a beautiful home, friends (that she doesn't get to see enough, but she has them), and a supportive extended family. She "has it all."

But, she doesn't feel that way. She doesn't *feel* much of anything. She's too rushed. Too tired. Going through the motions too much to stop and assess what's working, what's not working, where she is, where she wants to go.

I've been Jane. Maybe you have. Maybe you feel like her now. And in speaking with so many people over the years about this topic, I've met so many Janes (and a lot of Johns). We're everywhere. **We're tired. We're burned out. We're running on fumes.**

Are you going from activity to activity, meeting to meeting, responsibility to responsibility at such a pace that you barely have time to come up for air, take a pause, and ask yourself, "Is there a better way? And, if there is a better way (there is!—we'll get there shortly), how in the heck do I get there?"

Pause. Take time for yourself. Read this book. Do the exercises. This is your start.

If so, this book is for you. And you get to that "better way" by doing this. Pause. Take time for yourself. Read this book. Do the exercises. You'll also get there by stopping thought patterns, habits, and routines that are getting in your way. You get there by acknowledging where you are and where you want to go. I know that not one more thing can fit on your to-do list. I know you're exhausted. You're struggling, and you simply *cannot* take on one more thing.

You don't have to.

There Is Another Way

If you relate to Jane, if you have wondered whether there's more to life and just can't figure out how to make it all happen, I'm here to tell you that not only is there another way, there is a *better* way, and—though you may not *yet* be accustomed to thinking this way—**you deserve it.** And, believe it or not, it is within reach.

There is a way to get off the hamster wheel of life, out of the monotonous, repetitive, and unfulfilling routine or lifestyle that you may live. You can get out of the cycle of mundane activities, of going through the motions without experiencing personal growth or fulfillment. You can implement personal goals and see progress over time, pursuing your passions, dreams, and your deeper sense of purpose instead of just meeting basic needs and obligations.

There is another way you can break out of burnout. Constantly running on the aforementioned hamster wheel without breaks or changes leads to physical and emotional burnout from being exhausted and mentally drained by the repetitiveness and monotony. **You can change that.**

There is another way, one that gives you autonomy. One that makes you recognize *you're* in control—at least, much more in control than you may realize.

That's how *Hard Stop* can help. In this book, you'll work on ways to break free from feeling like you're constantly moving, but never moving forward. It will involve a lot of self-reflection and setting your priorities, which will help you make *intentional* choices about your life, set meaningful goals, and take steps to pursue a more fulfilling and purpose-driven life. It is going to require you to step out of your comfort zone and reflect deeply on your life as it is now to determine what's working—and what's not. It's going to require you to take the time to be clear about where you want to go and to set goals to help you get there. It's going to require holding yourself accountable to those goals by doing regular self check-ins to make sure you're on the path that you want to be on. It's going to ask you to look at activities, habits, behaviors, and relationships that you have in your life, and to assess which ones need a "hard stop" so that you can start living your best life.

This book is for you if you're ready and want to learn how to implement changes into your life to live more fully. This is *not* a philosophy book. It's not a psychology book. If you're looking for a rich discussion on the contemporary philosophical research on intentionalism from an empirical standpoint, or want to learn more about Franz Brentano, the German philosopher and psychologist generally regarded as the originator of modern intentionalism, please put this book down. You will be disappointed. This book is

> This book is for you if you're ready and want to learn how to implement changes into your life to live more fully.

100% for those of us who feel frustrated and want **practical** tips on how to change that.

There are intentionality experts that focus on breathwork, energy work, and other forms of breaking down internal barriers to discover internal joy and fulfillment. This book also does not get into these areas. On my own journey, I am not yet on this path, but recognize this is an approach others take—and it's effective and worth a deeper look if it speaks to you.

In my own intentionality journey, I'm very much drawn to what is important to me, how can I make time for those priorities, and what I need to get out of my own way so I can do them.

My focus is on *practical* intentionality, so on a practical note, here's how you will use this book.

- You'll start with your "why." Your North Star. Why are you doing this work in the first place?
- You'll assess where you are now, what's working for you, and what's not working for you across many areas of your life.
- You'll be introduced to the concepts of intentionality and mindset to help you plan your next steps.
- You'll learn about some habits and actions that get in the way of most people living their most fulfilling lives so you can be aware of and stop them if they apply to you.
- Then I'll give you the tools to help you, on a very practical level, start visualizing changes in your life, set your priorities, your boundaries, and help you get on your intentional path to start living the life you want to live.
- Throughout the book, you'll be asked to pause to reflect on the *gratitude* that you have for what

already exists in your list (and become more mindful of noticing the things you're thankful for on a regular basis).

While reading the book, you will note sections that invite you to go to the corresponding website to download templates or worksheets. For each of these, you'll go to www.ginaboedeker.com and select the corresponding chapter to find the appropriate pages.

I encourage you to not just quickly read through the "Hard Stop" and "Reflect" sections, but grab a journal dedicated to these exercises and a pen and take the time to invest in your own development. You picked up this book for a reason. You made the time to be here, right now, reading this book. So *be here.*

I'll be sharing some personal stories and some stories from other people I've met along my journey to help with both application and inspiration, **but this book isn't about me, nor is it about them. It's about *you* and where you want to go.** So make yourself the priority and get as much out of this book as you can by taking the time to do the work throughout.

Why "Hard Stop?"

Is there anything more respected in business than a "hard stop?"

"Hey everyone, I just want to let you all know that I have a hard stop at 11:00."

"No problem, I have a hard stop, too."

"Well let's get started, then, because we all have hard stops at the top of the hour."

We hear it **all. The. Time.** We know exactly what it means when we hear it. And we *respect* it. It's an *instant boundary*.

"I have to be out of this meeting at exactly this time for the next thing."

What would you wager that, 99% of the time, the hard stop is for another meeting?

We respect the boundaries that come with a hard stop so we can get our back-to-back meetings in, as many as possible, in a work day.

Hearing that phrase about 8,000 times in my life made me realize how much we respect other people's time and other people's priorities—and how we push ours to the side.

What would our reaction be if we heard someone say, "I have a hard stop because..."

- I have a yoga class.
- I'm taking a power nap to reset.
- I'm going on a hike to think for an hour.
- (Fill in the blank with another priority.)

What would your reaction be if someone was candid about what matters to them outside of making it, right on time, to yet another meeting? Would it warrant the same level of respect? You may want to go on a hike, but that can wait, right?

What would our lives look like if we were clear on our priorities and we were honest about them, not just

with ourselves, but with other people, so that we could set boundaries and have time for those priorities?

That's why this book exists. That's why "hard stop."

Time is finite, and how we spend our hours becomes how we spend our days, which becomes how we spend our months, our years, and our *lives*.

If you want to be able to live your life as fully as possible, you need to know what your goals *are,* you need to prioritize those goals along with the other responsibilities you have in your life, and you need to put boundaries up to ensure that you—and others—will respect those boundaries. You may need to stop doing some things in order to start others and to stay on this path.

Are you ready to get started?

I am.

Let's start on your "*why*."

> Time is finite, and how we spend our hours becomes how we spend our days, which becomes how we spend our months, our years, and our *lives*.

Chapter 1

Start with Why

"Your beliefs become your thoughts, your thoughts become your words, your words become your actions, your actions become your habits, your habits become your values, your values become your destiny."

– Mahatma Gandhi

I waited three and a half weeks to hear one word. Benign.

Those three weeks were the longest of my life. I felt every one of those thirty-four thousand minutes that made up the twenty four days. I'll spare you the details, but know that it included a large mass where one shouldn't have been, tears in my doctor's eyes as she ran out of the room to find a specialist, and symptoms I was experiencing that made us think I was dealing with a very bad prognosis. Sitting in that doctor's office, I had the immediate and profound realization that absolutely *everything* can change in a moment.

In those three weeks, my thoughts went dark. Very dark.

- How many birthday videos do I want to make for my kids? I don't want them to ever run out, so maybe I should make them until they're 100?

- I don't want my daughter to have to have a conversation with her dad about what to expect when she starts her period. I'll make that video. What else should I break down topically to tell her about? What about my son? What does he need to hear specifically from his mom?
- I mentally drafted a letter to the woman that my husband would eventually marry, asking her to love my babies. This one almost broke me.
- I had questions. So many questions. How could I ensure my kids would carry on without me, while still having the type of support I gave them? How could I set up my husband for a life post-me? How could I help people move on when inevitably, they would need to?

At this point you may be saying to yourself, "Woah, Gina. That sounds like a lot. Sorry to hear about your experience. But, what does this have to do with *Hard Stop*?"

Great question, thank you. Since you asked, I'll tell you. **Absolutely everything.**

In those three weeks I realized something profound that has stayed with me since then, and that realization was the impetus for writing this book.

I do not have one iota of regret.

In those three weeks, I kept coming back to this thought. Whatever was going to happen, I knew that I had no regrets about the life I was living, and, thankfully, in the most stressful time of my life, I didn't have to contend with regret on top of everything else. This was a comfort to me when I needed it.

I realized that I didn't have regrets for the life I was living because I have been very intentional about my priorities, my goals, and the type of life that I want to live, and spent every day focused on those intentions. I was living in a city of my *choosing*, with a family of my *choosing*, working in a business of my *choosing*. *Choice* reverberated for me in those weeks. I *chose* this life and I built it. Intentionally.

I didn't start off living intentionally. I went home right after college, having completed a major in an area I wasn't sure how to leverage in my favor. I had never really given any thought into what I wanted in my life. I fell in love with the guy in high school and we started our life together after college graduation.

Just a few months after our wedding, I started feeling discontent, though, initially, I couldn't pinpoint exactly what was wrong. I was working all day, coming home to an empty apartment (because he worked nights), eating dinner alone, and falling asleep while watching TV. I wasn't focused on my physical health and gained weight. I was going through the motions. That's really the only way I can explain it. This nagging feeling started popping up more and more regularly, and then never stopped, asking me *"Is this it? Is this your life? Is this all it's going to be?"*

And I knew I had to change. I wasn't sure how, exactly, but I knew I needed to.

I bought a five subject notebook and filled it with goals that I wanted to accomplish, places in the world I wanted to visit—at this point, I didn't even have a passport— experiences I wanted to have. In doing this work, much of which you'll also do in the coming chapters, I realized there was a lot I needed to change in myself. I discovered habits I had to unlearn in order to start on my desired path forward. Ultimately, I realized that I wasn't in the kind of relationship that was right for me at that time, and, more importantly, wouldn't be the right relationship for the person I was becoming. I left. I decided to leave St. Louis, Missouri, and moved to New York City, where I lived for the next fifteen or so years. It's where I met my now husband, where I started my family, built up my career, and then started my own company. I started living my "why."

Let me explain "why" a bit further. "Start with Why" is a concept popularized by author and leadership expert Simon Sinek in his book and TED Talk of the same name. The idea behind "Start with Why" is that successful individuals and organizations should begin by defining their core purpose or reason for existence—their "why"—before moving on to the "how" and "what" of their actions or products. I have implemented many of these lessons in my business (even including a "why" slide when explaining who we are and what we do at The Boedeker Group), but I found starting with "why" is critical for building the *life* you want to live as well.

When I was leaving my hometown in search of a different life, my "why" was experiencing the fullness of life, finding joy in every day (well, most days, anyway). Finding contentment. Finding myself.

But, as you'll learn as you work through these pages, living intentionally isn't a one and done experience. You're *constantly* reassessing where you are, where you want to be, what's in your way to get there, how you'll get there. When I was living in a crappy walk-up in the Upper East Side in Manhattan at twenty-five, that fit where I was at that time in my life. I was content then and there in that moment, but my goal wasn't to be living in that same crappy apartment, still using a dorm room fridge, in a space where I could put my feet on my bed from my couch, years later. I could enjoy the moment I was in while **working towards where I wanted to be next.**

My "why" has stayed consistent; wanting to live life to the fullest, finding joy in the everyday, making memories and having meaningful connections with my family, having adventures and new experiences, and creating a work environment that allows for the pursuit of these other goals. After being in a role as a senior

> I could enjoy the moment I was in while **working towards where I wanted to be next.**

leader in a Fortune 500 company, I found myself in a place where I knew that I wasn't living my "why." I had worked long and hard to get to where I was, and, on paper, everything was perfect. Just like Jane in the opening, on paper, all was as it "should" have been. I was at a company I loved with a team I was proud to be a part of. I enjoyed my work. I was in a good marriage and had a nice apartment, two beautiful babies, and the job I had strived for for years. But, I had that nagging feeling again. Something was missing.

I was getting up early to get time with my then one- and three-year-old children before going into work all day, getting home with just enough time to make dinner, eat with them, give them baths, and put them to bed. No time for my partner. No time for myself. I was running on fumes and just going through the motions. I wasn't the mom I wanted to be. I wasn't the leader I wanted to be. I wasn't the partner I wanted to be.

But I knew how to get out of it. I'd made big changes before. I knew I could do it again, if needed. I got a new notebook, got a pen, and started doing the work. What's working in my life now? What isn't? What do I want my relationship with my spouse to look like? What do I want professionally? What does it mean to be a mom on my terms? For months, I wrote it all out and started picturing what I wanted in the next phase of my life.

Shortly after starting this work, I filled out forms to create The Boedeker Group. A couple of months after filling out those forms, I left my role as managing director at a global publishing company and my team to start this new phase of my career. I was terrified. I was the most unlikely entrepreneur I knew. But my "why" wasn't being fulfilled. I wanted to live life to the fullest, to have meaningful experiences and adventures, and to find contentment in each and every day. I realized that I wanted more time to have those experiences with the people who mean the most to me, and being a mom on my terms was enough motivation to get over the massive fear of failure I had regarding launching a new business.

It all started with my "why."

Start with *Your* Why

I will cover the "whats" and "hows" of intentionality, setting boundaries, and putting in "hard stops" so you can live your best life.

Before that, though—here's your first assignment! You need to spend some time on *your* "why." Perhaps your "why" is to travel the world. Maybe being a present parent lights you up. Your "why" is not my "why," but we all have one, even if it takes a bit to uncover it. Understanding "why" you feel compelled to do this work in the first place will empower you to work toward the life you want to build. I spent a lot of time giving examples of the above to help provide clarity as to what it can feel like when you're not living your "why," and what can happen when you own it.

So, get out your pen and journal and give this some thought.

Stop and Reflect

1. Why are you doing this work now?
2. What are your motivations?
3. How do you hope living with intentionality will impact your life?
4. What is your "why?"
5. Write out what brings you gratitude right now at this moment in your life.

I know my "why," and by knowing my "why" and building my life around it intentionally, I was able to confront the terrifying situation I referenced at the start of this chapter and feel no regret about where I was in my life. It was an amazing realization, and it is my "why" for writing this book. I want you to have that feeling (without the scare, of course). I want

I want you to be able to experience the contentment that comes with an intentional life.

you to be able to start living your life more fully. I want you to be able to experience the contentment that comes with an intentional life.

So, now you know my "why." You're working on yours. Let's dive into the self-reflection questions to get yourself on the path to where you want to be.

Chapter 2

Making You the Priority

"You can't pour from an empty cup."

– Anonymous

Remember Jane? She spends her days making everyone else the priority. Her kids, her employees, her bosses, her partner. Her day fills up with other people's activities, priorities, deadlines, meetings, and, by the end of the day, she typically finds that she has not only has not made time for herself, *she hasn't even thought to do so.*

We're hearing more about the importance of self-care now than we ever used to. If your family is anything like mine, this was just not in our vernacular growing up. I don't remember my parents and grandparents regularly talking about their feelings about all of their responsibilities. I don't remember hearing it at all. Maybe it was because I was a kid. Maybe it was because they just got shit done. That's how it was.

But times were also different. While my parents both had steady jobs throughout my childhood, they also had a hard stop time at the end of the day where there was no expectation that they would be available to their company 24/7. They didn't work on weekends. They weren't catching up on emails during my soccer games. They weren't taking calls in the hallways of my music performances. They didn't have flexibility in their professional lives, but they had clear boundaries. It was a different time.

Today's world is exhausting. Really exhausting, at times. So many of us are not inclined to stop and think about how *we're* feeling about it all. We just roll up sleeves, make those lunches, and move on.

Enough.

It's time to say "enough."

It's time, even if it's uncomfortable—yes, I'm talking to you—to start thinking about *you*. To get into a habit of checking in with yourself about all the areas of your life and assessing what's working for you, what's not, what your goals are. It's time to start making you the priority, because only then, only when your cup is full, can you truly help others.

A friend of mine said to me, "I need to stop giving the best parts of myself to everyone else and leaving the leftovers for me."

A-men.

> "I need to stop giving the best parts of myself to everyone else and leaving the leftovers for me."

You may not be all the way "sold" yet. Why is it so hard for us to be self-reflective and give ourselves this time? Lots of reasons. Place a check next to the ones below that resonate with you.

Stop and Reflect

- **Busyness.** Your life is fast-paced and demanding. You may feel overwhelmed by work, family responsibilities, daily tasks which leave little time—or mental space—for self reflection.
- **Avoidance of discomfort.** It's real. So real that you will read a later chapter called "Dealing with Your Answers." Self-reflection can bring up uncomfortable feelings and thoughts. It's scary confronting our flaws, past mistakes, or unresolved issues, which makes it difficult to engage in deep introspection.
- **Lack of awareness.** You're reading this book, so you may have some inkling about the benefits of self-reflection, but not everyone has been exposed to the concept. Not everyone understands how self-reflection can improve their lives.
- **Distractions.** How often in the course of five minutes do you reach for your phone? It's become a recurring distraction for many of us. The prevalence of smartphones, social media, and constant connectivity can make it difficult to unplug and engage in this type of work. It's easy for these distractions to fill every spare moment, leaving little to no time for self-reflection.
- **Resistance to change.** Doing this work, *really* doing this work, can lead to insights that require changes in your behavior or lifestyle. People resist change. It's normal. It's more comfortable sometimes not to change, even when you recognize it's necessary for personal growth and well-being.

- **Lack of guidance.** Remember when I mentioned that I was raised in the '80s, in a family where no one ever talked about this stuff? I get it. Not everyone intuitively knows *how* to effectively engage in self-reflection or knows the questions to ask and may hesitate to start because of this. It may feel uncomfortable.
- **Fear of judgment.** Anyone think their partner, friends, or family may make fun of them for starting this path? It's normal. I've had these conversations. Many times. But you have to own and control what you need without fear of judgment. It's common to worry about how others will perceive your self-reflection. Will they think you're being self-indulgent? Self-absorbed? I don't know. Maybe they will. But don't let the fear of what others *may* think get in your way.
- **Lack of motivation.** It's hard to be motivated to engage in a practice if you don't have a clear understanding of its benefits, or have a sense of the purpose behind it. If this resonates with you, my hope is that reading more will help you see its value.
- **Fear of consequences.** A friend once shared with me that making this kind of time for herself was hard due to needing to free herself from all her other responsibilities. "Who else will do them? What will happen if I am not responsible for all of these things? Will my kid not have a winter coat that fits for the first cold day this year, because nobody else was thinking about it? Will we not have anything to pack for lunch because going to

the grocery store wasn't on *my* list? Will my managers think I'm not dedicated? Could I lose my job because of this other focus?"

What resonated above? How many did you check off? This is a big first step. Thanks for acknowledging what's hard for you. With that, you have now officially started the process of making yourself a priority. **Keep going.** Despite these challenges, self-reflection is an amazing tool for personal growth, decision-making, and overall well-being. Overcoming these obstacles often involves recognizing their existence (first step, check!), setting aside dedicated time for introspection (we'll focus on this in the next section), seeking support or guidance when needed, and understanding that self-reflection is a *process* that takes time and practice. It's also essential to approach self-reflection with self-compassion, acknowledging that it's okay to have flaws and areas for improvement. We all do.

Chapter 3

Self-Reflection: Starting the Process

"The more you seek the uncomfortable,
the more you will become comfortable."

– Conor McGregor

Starting something new is hard. It can be scary. It's certainly uncomfortable; I know this from experience. So, if you are not in a regular habit of implementing self-reflection in your life, welcome. I'm glad you're here and taking the time to work on yourself that you deserve.

As I shared in an earlier chapter, I'm passionate about this process. It's crazy to think I can pinpoint a trip to Walgreens as a turning point in my life, but I remember feeling lost, a bit aimless, and frustrated, without exactly knowing why. I decided to pick up a five subject spiral notebook and started spending time when I was alone in my house asking myself questions that I hadn't asked myself before. I didn't worry about what I would do with those answers— and you don't need to worry, either; we'll cover that in the next chapter. I didn't censor myself, probably for the first time in my life. I wasn't putting on a happy face and pretending all was well. It wasn't. Putting in the time to do this work helped me start figuring out what I was having a hard time articulating—what wasn't making me content in the life I was living, as well as what was. What brought me down? What brought me energy?

In this chapter, I'll share practical tools to help you get started on this practice, share some prompts and tools that have worked for me over the years, and help you make this one-off process into a regular routine. Here's the most important part. This is for you. 100%. If you don't like a question, skip it. If you think something isn't being asked that's important to you, write it down and answer it. Self-reflection is, by nature, a personal exercise, but these are tools to help so you're not on your own.

Set the Stage

Just like Jane won't be able to be fully present to do self-reflective work when she is regularly exhausted at 9:00 at night after chauffeuring people around, cooking dinner, doing dishes, doing all the *stuff* (which is the reason we need to make ourselves have a pause in the first place), **neither will you.**

You need to set the stage for your self-reflection process. Adapt for your needs and preferences, but here are some suggestions to make the time more effective.

- **Set aside dedicated time.** Does your schedule allow you to pick a certain day of the week or specific times during the day when you can be alone for a little while? If so, put the time in your calendar and treat it as you would any other appointment or commitment as you're getting into the practice. If there are days you feel more self-reflective and want to allocate more time for this activity, make good use of them, but the goal is to get into the habit of setting aside dedicated time for yourself, even if not a lot of time, to get started.

- **Choose a quiet, comfortable space.** Find a peaceful place where you can think without distractions. You don't need a room. It can be a corner of your home, a park, a quiet coffee shop—wherever you feel at ease. If you work in a busy office but take a lunch break, is there a local park or a quiet cafe where you can be alone in your thoughts for a bit? *Peace* and *quiet* are key.

- **Gather your tools.** Want to know one of the great parts about starting this process? **You don't need much!** A journal (or notebook) and a pen are really all you need to start. You may prefer digital tools, such as writing in a document on your computer or using a voice recorder. Whatever your chosen tools are, that's all you need.

- **Ask yourself guiding questions.** Especially when starting a new process, it's helpful to stimulate your self-reflection by asking yourself open-ended questions related to your goals, values, and areas of your life you want to explore. I'll provide a list of self-reflection questions in the next section, as well as additional questions to explore online for inspiration.

- **Journal or document your thoughts.** Write down your thoughts, feelings, and insights as you contemplate these questions. Sometimes feelings come out more than answers. Write what comes to you. Be honest with yourself. That's worth repeating: **be honest with yourself.** Don't worry about grammar, don't worry about structure. No one else is reading this. It's a personal exercise, completely for *you*.

- **Practice self-compassion.** Remember that you are doing this work for personal growth. The purpose of this exercise is not self-criticism. This isn't about blaming yourself if you're not where you want to be in certain areas of your life right now. Be kind and patient with yourself as you explore these thoughts and feelings. This is a new process for you; give yourself a break as you're going through it.

Over time, this practice can help you gain deeper self-awareness, make more intentional choices, and lead a more purposeful and fulfilling life. Make this a priority in your process and your schedule and ensure it remains a meaningful, sustainable part of your life.

> The key to self-reflection is consistency and authenticity.

Start High Level

I found it helpful to start at a high level when self-reflection was new to me, so if you haven't already set the stage for this work, take a moment to get your tools, find a quiet space, and be ready to start writing.

The question, **"Am I where I want to be in my life?"** is a great starting point. It can allow you to capture everything. Are you where you want to be in your life...

- In your romantic relationship?
- Professionally?
- Physically?
- Spiritually?
- Emotionally?
- Financially?
- As a parent?
- As a son/daughter?
- As a friend?
- In your community?

Are you where you want to be in your life right now?

Go there.

See it. *Feel* it. Even smell it, if you can.

Don't limit yourself. Let this be a stream of consciousness exercise. Not everything has to be "right." Not everything has to be fully thought out, it just needs to come out of your brain and onto paper. Sometimes, when it's not planned, when you don't try to write it out perfectly, when you aren't focused on editing before your pen hits the paper and you let yourself truly brainstorm, you may bring to the surface authentic thoughts you didn't realize were there.

So, go there. I'll be here when you come back. Take all the time you need.

Naming Your Priorities

If you want to gain clarity and start making more intentional choices, you have to know what, exactly, your priorities are. We'll keep the flow of self-reflection going, and work through a step-by-step process to help you do this.

Brainstorm your priorities. Set a timer for five minutes, grab a pen and paper — or your computer — and limit the distractions around you. List out all the priorities you have in your life. Think about categories like family, career, health, personal development, relationships, hobbies, and community involvement. List out everything that comes to mind. A best practice in brainstorming is to not limit yourself (more is usually better) and build on the ideas you put forward. A woman in her mid-forties, Jaime, was starting this process, completed this exercise, and came up with the following list:

- Miguel (her spouse)
- Julia (daughter)
- Fernando (son)
- Family time – four of us together
- Extended family/in-laws
- Nature
- Friendships
- Learning Spanish
- Physical fitness
- Community
- Building her business
- Creating a comfortable home environment
- Financial stability
- Volunteering /giving back

- Mental health
- Travel
- Becoming well-read
- Cultural awareness
- Learning the piano
- Making time for herself

Naturally, her partner and children rated higher than learning how to play the piano. But as she did this exercise, she didn't limit herself. Don't limit yourself as you do it, either. Just get it all out. What do you want to prioritize in your life?

- **Categorize your priorities.** After you have captured a long list of your priorities, group them into broader categories to make the list more manageable and organized. For example, you might have categories like "health and well-being," "career and financial," "relationships," and "personal growth."

Below are some examples of what *could* fit within various categories. Don't feel stifled or limited by these, and also don't think "well, I really *should* have a priority in this category." If you do, you do. If you don't, you don't. These are shared only to help you think as big as you can in this process. If you see any individual priorities that didn't make your list but resonate with you, consider adding them at this time. If they don't resonate with your priorities, ignore them.

Personal Growth and Development
- Self-awareness
- Self-improvement
- Lifelong learning
- Emotional intelligence

Spirituality and Mindfulness:
- Meditation
- Mindfulness
- Gratitude
- Higher purpose-seeking

Relationships
- Partner/Spouse
- Family
- Friends
- Colleagues
- Social connections

Career and Professional Development
- Career goals
- Skill development
- Work-life balance
- Time management

Health and Well-being:
- Physical health
- Mental health
- Fitness and exercise
- Nutrition
- Sleep

Financial Management:
- Budgeting
- Saving and investing
- Debt management
- Financial goals

Creativity and Hobbies:
- Pursuing creative interests
- Engaging in hobbies and passions
- Finding joy and fulfillment in leisure activities

Life Purpose and Meaning:
- Identifying one's purpose
- Finding meaning in everyday life
- Contributing to society
- Effecting philanthropic acts

Time Management and Productivity
- Goal setting
- Prioritization
- Effective time management
- Elimination of distractions

Environment and Sustainability
- Creating a conducive living and working environment
- Learning sustainable living practices
- Reducing environmental impact

Communication Skills
- Effective communication
- Active listening
- Conflict resolution
- Build meaningful relationships

Personal Values and Ethics:
- Defining personal values
- Making ethical decisions
- Living in alignment with values

Life Transitions:
- Coping with change and uncertainty
- Navigating major life transitions (e.g., marriage, parenthood, retirement)

Community and Social Impact
- Community involvement
- Philanthropy
- Social responsibility

Travel and Exploration
- Exploring new places and cultures
- Broadening one's perspective through travel

Self-Care and Well-being Practices
- Self-care routines
- Stress management
- Emotional well-being

Education and Personal Knowledge
- Participating in lifelong learning
- Expanding personal knowledge and skills

Goal Setting and Achievement:
- Setting both short and long-term goals for personal and professional aspirations
- Tracking progress on goals

Technology and Digital Detox:
 - *Balancing technology use*
 - *Learning to practice digital detoxes and mindfulness in the digital age*

Cultural and Artistic Appreciation:
 - *Cultural experiences*
 - *Art, music, and literature appreciation*

- **Reflect on each priority.** Reflecting on your priorities can help you gain deeper insights into yourself and help you make more intentional choices regarding how you allocate your time, energy, and resources. **This is important work.** Take time to reflect on each priority individually. If you have a long list, this is going to take some time. And by "this can take some time," I mean that this process alone could take you *weeks*, if not longer. For each of your priorities, perhaps you can make a goal of thinking through it and journaling on it daily for twenty minutes a day until you get through them all. When I shared this activity with a friend, she said she loved it and found it helpful, but found herself feeling slightly overwhelmed. If you are feeling the same way at this point, simply acknowledge it and make a plan to get through it in a timeframe that works for you. You can continue reading, but come back to this exercise until you've had the opportunity to really think through these. Most importantly: **Don't rush this part.** Consider why you wrote each priority down and ask yourself the following questions for each item on your list:

o   Why is this priority important to me?
o   How does this priority align with my values or beliefs?
o   What impact does this priority have on my overall well-being and happiness?
o   Does focusing on this priority enhance my sense of fulfillment and contribute positively to my life?
o   What else do I feel when I think about this priority?

- **Assign a rating to each priority.** Rating your priorities provides you with a clear and concise way to distinguish the relative importance of each priority you listed (giving you an at-a-glance view into which priorities are most important to you). When you have a clear understanding of your hierarchy of priorities, you can direct your efforts to those that you rate the highest and allocate more time and attention to what truly matters to *you*. Use a scale of one to five. A higher rating indicates a higher importance.
- **Prioritize within categories.** Prioritizing within categories provides a framework for making intentional choices and finding balance in your life (or at least harmony, if not balance). The goal is to give appropriate attention to various aspects of your life while focusing on what matters most within each category. For example, Jaime bucketed learning piano and becoming fluent in Spanish

together as "Personal Development." Given that her husband's family lives in Mexico, she prioritizes being fluent in Spanish more than revisiting *Ode to Joy.* She wants to do both, but when time is a factor and she has to make choices, she knows she needs to spend time on self-development and may give more time to Spanish. That's where this helps. Take time to prioritize within your categories. Identify which priorities have the highest ratings within each category.

- **Create your master list.** Have you ever had a list of all of your priorities in one place, rated by what's most important to you and what will get the most of your time and attention? No? **Well, now's the time to make that list.** Write it out, print it out, put it in a place that you can see it daily. These are *your* priorities, and, for that reason, these are worth revisiting every day. There's a "Master List" worksheet on the website you can fill in, or which you can use the structure of to format this section of your own journal.

- **Fill in the pie.** A simple image of a pie that's broken into slices can be a powerful visual depicting the allocation of time to your priorities. I've found it helpful to create two of these. One is where I think I am *now*: what's the biggest piece of the pie? What's getting most of my time and energy? I also like to create one that's more aspirational, more aligned with how I'd *want* the pie to look. Simply draw a circle and create the wedges, like the example below. You can see in the image that I labeled priorities that are important to me and I want to track, and then I rank, on a scale of 0 (not where I want it to be) to 10 (goal), where I am with regard to my goal. You will write down the topics around your pie—*you* determine what's important to put on there—to easily get a visual representation of how you rate your satisfaction in the areas more important to you.

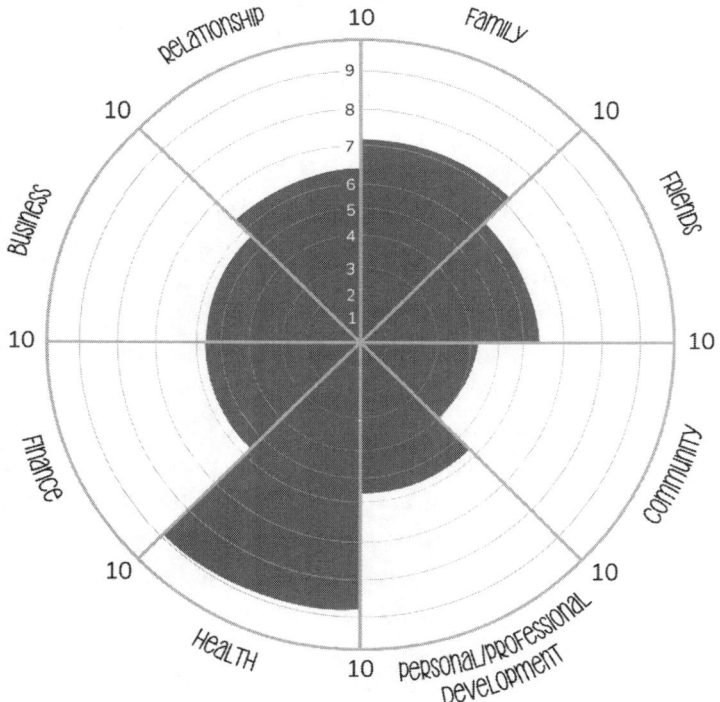

- **Evaluate balance.** When you wrote out your list, did you find that you were unbalanced in any particular categories? This is your list, so the recommendation isn't to make changes, necessarily, but you may want to consider whether you're overly focused on one area of life to the detriment of others. Balance isn't always possible, but striving to move *towards* it can help lead to a fulfilling and well-rounded life. What categories have the highest number of priorities listed? What categories have the least—or don't show up at all? What are your thoughts on this imbalance? Does that work for you, or is that something you want to change?

Priorities will change over time as your life circumstances change, and that's okay. It's expected! We are not spending the time in this section talking about how to regularly revisit and adjust your priorities. We'll do that in a later chapter. For now, accept the virtual high-five I'm giving you for this work. If you took the time to work through the exercises, I know it was a lot. Take a break, come back fresh, and then we'll move on to some more self-reflective work about where you are in your life now that we have your priorities identified, printed—they're printed, right?—and in view for you to revisit regularly.

Where Are You Now?

In later chapters, I will help you identify where you want to go, set goals, and picture your life differently based on what's most important to you and most aligns with your values. I found that trying to picture that vision of my life *first* was harder for me than stopping and assessing where I was in the moment and being reflective about life as it was. If your mind works differently, and working on mindset and setting intentions for your future would be a better start for you, I welcome you to go to Chapter Six, "Visioning Change." Otherwise, here, you'll again need your self-reflection tools to start answering some guiding questions about your life as it is right now.

Below are questions intended to help you start assessing where you are *now* so you can work on determining where you want to go. As before, there are a lot of questions; each one may take you a little while. **Don't rush this part.** Break these into a few questions at a time, journal your responses, and then we'll move on to how to address these answers in the next chapter.

Do not limit or edit yourself in this exercise.

Stop and Reflect

- How are my relationships with family, friends, and significant others at this moment?
- What are my most important roles and responsibilities at this moment? (e.g. parent, employee, student, friend, partner)
- What brings me joy, fulfillment, and a sense of purpose?
- What aspects of my life do I feel the most content about and grateful for right now?

- Am I satisfied with my current environment and living situation?
- What are my current financial circumstances? Am I managing my finances effectively?
- What are the most significant challenges or obstacles I'm currently facing?
- How do I currently spend my time? Is this aligned with my goals and values?
- What are the daily habits and routines that shape my life right now? Are they serving me well?
- Do I feel a sense of purpose or direction in my life right now, and if so, what is it?
- What is my current level of self-awareness? How can I improve it?
- What is my current level of physical health? Am I taking care of my body adequately?
- What are my current interests, hobbies, and passions?
- How am I spending my time on a daily and weekly basis?
- What are the key strengths and weaknesses I bring to my personal and professional life?
- What are the main sources of stress or unhappiness in my life? How can I mitigate or manage them?
- How do I perceive my own personal growth and development at this moment?
- What support systems do I have in my life?
- What makes me feel the most grateful in my life right now?

Stopping to reflect on how you're feeling at *this* moment in time is one of the most impactful parts of living a more intentional life.

Acknowledging what makes you happy and grateful, as well as what doesn't bring you joy (or downright brings stress, anxiety, or unhappiness), is important to recognize. Your responses to these questions will help you shape where you want to go next. That will come in a later chapter. For now, we'll move on to how to deal with your answers if any aren't sitting well.

Stopping to reflect on how you're feeling at *this* moment in time is one of the most impactful parts of living a more intentional life.

Chapter 4

Dealing with Your Answers

"When I accept myself just as I am, then I can change."

– Carl Rogers

You spent the last chapter starting an honest dialogue with yourself. You began acknowledging what is working well for you in your life, and paused to reflect on what isn't. It's uncomfortable, I know. When I started doing this work and began asking myself and answering these questions, I admittedly wanted to edit myself—*what if someone reads this!?*—I wanted to gloss over the parts I didn't like and reflect solely on what was going well in my life. I felt like I was just complaining, otherwise, and don't other people have it way worse? I kept up a cheery outside disposition even when I knew I wasn't happy, because I didn't want other people to know what I was struggling with, and I've been terrified to put on paper the things about my life I wanted to change, because I knew that was the first step in holding myself accountable to *do* something about it.

And that's scary.

No one else was reading my journal. No one else could do this work for me. Once I committed to doing it, I knew I would be the one who would have to do something about it.

> **If you're feeling discomfort now, it's completely normal.**

So, I want to take a moment now to acknowledge that discomfort now in case you are feeling it. It's normal if you are.

If you're wondering, "What do I do with the fact that I'm unhappy with my spouse? What does it mean if I'm unfulfilled at work? I've said I'm inactive and not focusing enough on my personal health, does this mean I have to join a gym?"

Here's the good news. **You get to drive what you do next.** I'll provide some steps below to consider when you don't like your self-reflection answers and want to start addressing the issues, but know that only *you* will decide how and when you begin.

Like Sarah, you'll have a choice.

Sarah is in her mid forties. She is in a relationship that she explained to me as "fine." She is in a job that she will also say is… fine. She doesn't love her boss, but appreciates the consistent paycheck and likes her team. She has a good relationship with her friends. Her family lives close by. She has a house that she likes, that's hers, and when we first started these discussions, she said that things, up until that point, felt "fine." She honestly didn't think much about it.

Something started to shift for her, though. She couldn't pinpoint the *exact* moment when she started to feel differently. It wasn't the lightbulb or "Eureka!" kind of moment. It was nothing like that. It rarely is. She said it felt more like a nagging feeling that something just felt off. Something she couldn't easily name but was just, "ugh" (how she said it).

Have you been there? Has something not felt completely right, but you're not sure exactly how to put it into words? And you're not sure what changed? You're not sure why you're feeling this way?

I met Sarah (name changed for confidentiality) years ago, and our paths have crossed a number of times since then. When we were in touch last year and she said things were "ugh," I shared with her that trying to be more intentional had such a profound impact on me and said, "I don't know if this will work for you, but it did for me. Want me to share more about it?"

So, I did. I shared with her what I shared with you in the last chapter, acknowledging that simply admitting something is off and giving herself that time to reflect was a huge step in a direction that could be really impactful. Much to her credit (and yours, for being here, making the time to do this work as well), she started. She bought a journal and committed to writing in it at least ten minutes a day. I never held her feet to the fire. I don't know if she did it every day, but she told me she was "keeping up with it."

Sarah said she started capturing what was bringing her happiness, as well as what wasn't. She used the list of self-reflective questions to ask herself things she had never asked herself. She wrote down goals that she had that she hadn't vocalized before. She thought about the places she wanted to visit that she hadn't seen, books she wanted to read, and experiences she wanted to have. Her "fine" became "not fine" when she decided she wanted more.

That's the important piece here. *She* got to decide what changes she wanted to make. She had choices, and **she felt empowered by them.**

I think we would both love to be able to say she found out what wasn't bringing her joy and, with a snap of her fingers, was able to change everything. That wouldn't be accurate, though. That's not how this process usually goes.

> It's empowering to know you have a *choice*.

She's in it. Right now, she's in it. And she was open to having me share this story because she knows she isn't alone and doesn't want other people to feel alone if they're "going through it."

She's still deciding what she wants to do about the relationship she's in. She says it feels more like a convenience at times than a true partnership, but she's finding it hard to just leave because there's history there. Maybe a bit of dependence. Even if it's not *perfect*, she has *someone*. She's still feeling that and is unsure as to exactly what she wants to do about it.

She is still at her company and on the same team (these changes don't always happen quickly), but said she is feeling motivated because she's actively looking for another group within the company to join, and just knowing that there are other options, even if she hasn't moved on yet, makes the day-to-day a bit better when her boss is on her nerves. That piece hasn't changed.

And—this one is done already!—she went on a trip by herself for the first time. She was, in her own words, "nervous as hell," but did it anyway, and said it opened up the desire to do so again.

I give her a ton of credit because she didn't allow herself to live with "fine." She didn't allow the fear of asking herself those tough questions to get in her way.

Because asking yourself tough questions is scary, you may think:

"I don't want to leave my relationship!"

"I don't want to confront my boss!"

"I don't want to travel alone! I don't want to *be* alone!"

Of course you may not want those things. Sarah's still figuring out how she wants to handle her own responses. That was *her* story. She's making these decisions for *her*.

> You will decide what decisions **you** want to make.

You will decide what decisions **you** want to make.

If you say that you're not happy in your relationship, it doesn't mean you have to leave it. If you're unhappy in your job, you don't have to quit. Acknowledging you're not happy doesn't mean you need to make a drastic change, but it *does* allow you to start making the changes that you feel are appropriate, such as having honest conversations with your partner, opening up to your boss—if needed—about where you want to go professionally, and start making what you're not happy with a priority again if it hasn't been and you acknowledge that you want it to be.

This is what gets you off the treadmill of day-to-day activities that are being done without you actively working towards goals in areas that are important to you. That's all. No one is asking you to leave your spouse, or move from your hometown, or quit your job. **Only you will decide what to do next.**

Below are some steps to consider when you don't love your self-reflection answers, and you are ready to start addressing those issues.

- **Acknowledge your feelings.** It's natural to feel uncomfortable or dissatisfied when you uncover areas in need of improvement. Acknowledge these feelings *without judgment.* You're doing the work. Know that these feelings are part of the self-reflection process and you can't make changes without acknowledging them. So, go you!
- **Practice self-compassion.** We talk *way* more harshly to ourselves than we would some of our worst enemies. Acknowledge that inner voice and try to make the shift to be more kind and compassionate towards yourself. **Self-reflection is a tool for growth, not self-criticism.** Treat yourself as a friend who is seeking to improve. How would you talk to them? Talk to yourself the same way.
- **Identify specific areas.** You worked through a lot of categories in your self-reflection questions. Are there any specific areas of your life in which you identified you're the most unhappy or dissatisfied? Clarify what needs to improve or change.
- **Practice patience.** Change takes time. Setbacks are part of the process. Be patient with yourself and understand that growth is a journey, and it's gradual. Don't give up if things aren't moving quickly. Know they won't, necessarily. Accept that.

- **Stay accountable.** Admitting what's not working in your life is just the first step. As we put plans in place in future chapters, stay accountable to them—they'll be *your* goals! Tracking your efforts is the best way to stay on track.
- **Practice self-care.** Prioritize well-being practices that support your personal growth journey. This includes managing stress, getting enough sleep, and being mindful of your mental and emotional health. Some people consider self-care to consist of spa treatments and getting their nails done. For others, it's a day of quiet: reading at home, getting outside, bingeing your favorite show for a few episodes, even calling a friend. Whatever your definition of self-care is, prioritize it.
- **Rely on professional services.** If dealing with your answers is too daunting, too much, too uncomfortable, or you simply don't know how to find your way forward, you're not alone. Don't hesitate to rely on professionals: coaches, therapists, and counselors are there to support you if you need it.
- Most importantly, remember that self-improvement is a lifelong process and it's okay to encounter challenges along the way. You just did your first honest assessment of all areas of your life since— when *did* you last do this? Have you *ever*? So, just sit with your responses and acknowledge that you may not yet know how to deal with your answers, but **you're starting a process**—an important one—that will serve you well going forward.

Stop and Reflect

1.   Which of your answers from the previous chapter are you struggling with the most?
2.   What concerns or worries do you have about these responses?
3.   Which of the strategies above are you going to commit to in order to help you move forward?
4.   What other strategies might you implement to help you deal with the answers you didn't love?

I purposefully excluded a recommendation I've heard others make regarding this topic: Seek support from your family and friends. I'll tell you why I omitted it, so you can decide for yourself.

When I first started this work, it was new, it was uncomfortable, and it was causing me to confront some pretty big feelings that I wasn't quite sure what to do with right away. When I realized how miserable I was in my first marriage, I knew I wasn't ready to share those feelings until I was more sure I knew what it meant for me and what I planned to *do* about those feelings. After filling up my five subject notebook, I felt confident in the direction I wanted to go, so I told people about the decisions I was making that were best for me. I was met with a tremendous amount of pushback. I had so many conversations with people telling me that things in *their* life weren't so great, but they weren't just going to leave. I had a lot of people telling me I was making a mistake. I had people telling me I would regret it.

I *wasn't* making a mistake. And I don't regret my decision.

Only *I* knew what was right for me, but when the feelings were still nascent and I was working through them, I wasn't ready to "defend" myself. Not immediately. Years later, those same people understand the decisions I made at the time and acknowledge that it was the best decision for me—but here's what's tough. People will filter your experiences through their *own* experiences, and their judgements of what you do (and don't do) will likely have more to do with *them* than they will have with you.

Others will say that reaching out to family, friends, and professionals can be a very valuable tool at this early stage, so if that will be helpful to you, consider that as well at this time for helping you in this process. However, give a lot of thought to the *right* people for you to open up to at this time. Be picky. Choose your tribe. This is extremely important. Because when it's new and vulnerable, you, too, may just need a listening ear and not a critic to whom you need to defend choices you are just starting to decide upon.

> People will filter your experiences through their *own* experiences, and their judgements of what you do (and don't do) will likely have more to do with *them* than they will have with you.

In this section, we have focused on developing a better understanding of where you are now. In the next few chapters, we'll switch gears a bit to focus on where you want to go. For now, big cheers to you for doing this work! It's a tremendous start, and you have no idea how much doing this work can not only impact your life, but inspire others who may be afraid to start their own. Yay you!

Chapter 5

Intentionality

"The road to success is paved with intentions acted upon."

– Unknown

Let's start with the basics. What is intentionality, and why am I writing a full book about the importance of living life more intentionally?

First, to answer the "why," I believe that living your life more intentionally leads to living a happier life. It's as simple as that for me—and it's more than enough motivation to make it a part of my day-to-day life. When you stop and reflect on where you are and where you want to be, you put yourself in control of your life. You feel more gratitude for what you have. You feel more focused on where you want to go. You infuse your thoughts, actions, and choices with purpose and meaning. You get off the path of navigating crazy, busy schedules—or at least you become cognizant that it's happening as a first step!—and chart the course that you want to be on, creating the life you want to live.

Living intentionally is *empowering*.

It's *empowering*.

I want you to feel this way. That's my hope for you.

Intentionality is not a new concept. Humans have long sought anchor points, seeking meaning and direction as they navigate the intricate currents of life. The roots of intentionality as a self-reflection method can be traced back across millennia, intertwined with various philosophical, spiritual, and psychological traditions. From the ancient Stoics, who championed the concept of living "in accordance with nature," to Eastern philosophies, such as Buddhism and Taoism, which emphasize mindfulness and the alignment of one's intentions with the natural flow of life, intentionality has been a cornerstone of wisdom and well-being. It's been a recurring theme in historical literature and meditative practices throughout history.

As part of my practice with intentionality, I've learned more about its history and practices. I've learned about philosophers like Aristotle, who believed the idea of intentionality is central to understanding human actions. I have read about Jean-Paul Sartre's idea of radical freedom, about the responsibility of individuals to make deliberate choices. I learned about Buddhist traditions that teach mindfulness meditation that involves being fully present in the moment and intentionally directing one's attention to breath, sensations, and thoughts. I know there's value in all of this, and know it's powerful to know about the historical and religious contexts. And it should fit within a chapter introducing the concept of intentionality.

I also know this:

That's not what Jane needs to hear about right now when she can't find five flippin' minutes for herself. She isn't going to happen upon concepts of intentionality in Buddhist writings or meander through *Being and*

Nothingness when she's fall-down tired at the end of the day, after making everyone else's priorities her own. The focus, to start, needs to be on why it's important to implement it into your life, and *practical* tips to get the process started.

Most people aren't building an intentionality practice in their day for all the reasons you checked off in Chapter Two, "Making You the Priority:"

- Busyness
- Avoidance of discomfort
- Lack of awareness
- Distractions
- Resistance to change
- Lack of guidance
- Fear of judgment
- Lack of motivation
- Lack of energy

That was you three chapters ago! If you have decided to pick up this book, have read to this point, and have completed the exercises in the previous chapter (it's not too late to turn back if you haven't), you have essentially laid a foundation for living an intentional life.

That's *huge*!

You now have the foundation for living intentionally. Now we'll focus on creating ongoing processes to keep you on this path.

Creating an Intentionality Practice

Creating an intentionality practice—because what we're doing is practicing: we're learning, implementing, and we'll evolve as we go—involves steps that naturally will depend on your personal preferences and goals. That said, here's a general framework that you can use to start building your practice. Don't work through these yet. We'll work on ranking your priorities in Chapter Eight, and there will be accompanying worksheets to help you. For now, just take in what building an intentionality practice entails:

- **Self-reflection.** You started this work already in Chapter Three. You reflected on what is and isn't working in your life right now. You journalled about what's most important to you, and what you want to achieve and change.
- **Set clear intentions.** We'll work to define specific intentions based on the self-reflection exercises you created. They will be clear, actionable, and aligned with your values. You may set your intentions related to work, relationships, personal growth, and well-being. We'll use the themes that will be introduced to you in Chapter Seven to help you create your intentions.
- **Prioritize your intentions.** Just as you prioritized what's most important in your life now, you will consider what's most important as you move forward and prioritize so that you won't overwhelm yourself with too many goals set at once. It's best to focus on a manageable number that you can realistically work on.

- **Mindful planning.** You'll plan your daily, weekly, monthly, and yearly activities with your intentions in mind. How can you incorporate intentional actions that align with your goals? How can you fit it all in? You'll create a schedule that reflects your priorities and assess your progress weekly to make sure you're on track.
- **Practice mindfulness.** Introduce mindfulness into your daily routine. This can include meditation, deep breathing exercises, or simply being present in the moment. Mindfulness helps you stay connected to your intentions.
- **Daily journaling.** That's right, daily. Record your intentions, daily actions, and reflections every day. Use your journal to help you stay on track. Writing down your experiences and observations can deepen your self-awareness and commitment to living intentionally.
- **Acknowledging gratitude.** Every day, write down at least three things that make you grateful. Try to go deep and really *feel* what makes you grateful. Shut your eyes, feel the abundance of what's good in your life, and take time to capture those moments. Instead of writing "my son," for example, I could write, "When writing this chapter, my son woke up, walked into my office with sleepy eyes and tousled hair, and just climbed into my lap to say 'Morning mom,' giving me a long, warm hug." See the difference? More importantly, *feel* it? I still can.
- **Accountability.** Once you are ready to do so, with whom can you share your intentions in your circle?

A friend, family member, mentor, mental health professional? Having someone who can hold you accountable and provide support and encouragement is priceless. Just keep in mind what I wrote earlier; the timing of this and who you choose to discuss your intentions with is important!

- **Review and adjust.** This is not a one-and-done process. Just know that going into it. You'll review your progress regularly to see if you're meeting your goals and staying true to your intentions. If—no, when—you find yourself deviating or facing challenges, you'll adjust your approach and reassess your intentions as you go.
- **Learn from setbacks.** You'll have them. It's normal. Acknowledge that setbacks and failures are a part of the process. Learn from them, rather than being discouraged.
- **Celebrate success.** Give yourself a high five when you reach your milestones, no matter how small those wins may seem. Recognizing your progress and your achievements can help reinforce your commitment to intentional living.

Most importantly, remember that your intentionality practice will be *yours*. You will tailor it to your specific needs and preferences. The key will be to regularly evaluate, adjust, and integrate intentional living into your daily life to align your actions with your values and goals.

This is what we'll work on in detail in a few chapters. For now, "Visioning Change" will help you think through *big* intentions and not limit yourself before you start this work!

Chapter 6

Visioning Change

*"Visualize this thing that you want, see it, feel it, believe in it.
Make your mental blueprint, and begin to build."*

– Robert Collier

There was a time that I couldn't see my life any other way.
I've already said that sometimes, it's just not part of our
daily habits to stop, reflect, and think about the life that we
want to live. So, yes, that was a part of it, but even when I
made the time to stop, reflect, and try to visualize changes,
the reality of my current situation made it such that trying
to see a different way was difficult for me. *Really* difficult.

I want to start this chapter by sharing my struggle in
this area because I know that envisioning change isn't
naturally easy for everyone when they start this kind of
work. Even for those who do it regularly, not all of us are
wired the same way, and this continues to be an area
that I struggle with. While some people gravitate towards
the vision and Pinterest boards, and seem to have where
they want to go all figured out (and are working towards
finding a way to get there), others have a tough time
even envisioning what types of materials should be used
for the board.

That's me.

When I was in a relationship with my ex, living in my hometown, I couldn't envision what it would look like to live in a different city, single, doing a different job. It wasn't a picture I could conjure up, at first.

When I was working in midtown Manhattan with two small kids at home, I couldn't envision a different future. Starting my own business was such a foreign concept that it wasn't even on my radar.

But there was a time when I allowed myself to envision (and vocalize) a *big* thought, something that would be a big change in my life. I had just had my second child, and my family was spending a month in Rio de Janeiro, Brazil, with my in-laws during my maternity leave from work. I remember saying to my husband, "I don't know how—or if—it's even possible with my job, but I'd love for us to find a way to spend a month here every year."

I was done having kids, which meant no more maternity leaves to have extended time off, and my vacation schedule was such that I didn't want to give it all up for one trip. I have my side of the family, too, and there are other places in the world we want to visit. It was such a big thought at the time, and it seemed impossible.

But once I said it, it was *out there*. Once I allowed myself to think about it, I couldn't stop thinking about it—but it was too big, too much of an "ask" in my life, so I kept putting it to the side. But the nagging feeling was always there. "Is it possible? *How* could it be possible?"

That maternity leave ended in January 2016. By October of that year, I had filed the paperwork to start The Boedeker Group.

Only once I allowed myself to envision a big change—to *really* see it, to start *feeling* it—could I start making the moves to make that vision a reality.

In the summer of 2023, after I launched *Hard Stop* (the newsletter), I wrote an article titled "What Seems Impossible?" It starts off like this:

> *I never thought I'd be able to make this work.*
>
> *It seemed like too big of a "wish"/too big of an ask, given the job and life I had at the time.*

And yet, here I am doing what I thought was impossible.

I go on to share that I was writing that article from an office in Rio de Janeiro that I rented for the month. My kids were with their grandparents, taking gymnastics, playing soccer, and having overnights with their cousins and aunts and uncles. We were meeting for lunch every day with the family. They were soaking up the culture and practicing their Portuguese. They were getting to know their dad's home in a way they never could with a couple of weeks of vacation here and there. They were *living* in another country, and they have been doing so every year since I started my business.

This exact story may not resonate with you. You may have zero interest in leaving your home once a year to live in another country for a month at a time. But the idea behind it is one we likely all can understand. We *all* have those things that seem too big, too unrealistic, "too much" for us to allow ourselves to really think they could some-how become our reality.

That's why visioning is important; it allows us to really picture—and *feel*, when we get good at it—differences in key areas of our lives.

The above is *why* visioning is important. But what exactly is it?

Visioning refers to the practice of creating vivid men-tal images or scenarios pertaining to your desired goals, experiences, and outcomes. It involves using your imagi-nation and sensory faculties to picture, in as much detail as possible, the life you want to lead, the achievements you aim to reach, and the person you aspire to become. The process of visioning allows you to mentally rehearse and create a compelling and motivating vision of your future. It can be a powerful tool for clarifying your goals, boosting motivation, and influencing your mindset and actions to align with your envisioned life.

In Chapter Three, "Self Reflection: Starting the Pro-cess," I introduced various categories you could consider employing when starting that work that may be helpful as you start envisioning your life. Use these categories simply as prompts to get you thinking; you don't have to visualize changes in each of these areas of your life. You are in the driver's seat and will prioritize where you want to start.

Stop and Reflect: Visioning Exercise

The below visioning exercise can be adapted to various areas of your life. It will help you envision your goals, build motivation, and mentally rehearse your desired outcome.

Adapt it for one specific area of your life to start, such as your career, relationships, health, or personal growth, and then you can continue using this same template in other areas. Take the time you need to complete it. You may not be able to get through this in one sitting. That's okay. Come back to it as needed, until you feel you could *vision* in detail. Let's start.

Preparation

- Find a quiet, comfortable place where you won't be disturbed.
- Sit or lie down in a relaxed position.
- Take a few deep breaths to calm your mind and body.

Focus on Your Goal

- Identify a specific goal or area of your life you want to visualize.

Create a Vivid Mental Image

- Close your eyes and start to imagine the desired outcome. Make the mental image as vivid as possible.
- Use all your senses. What do you see, hear, smell, taste, and feel in this scenario? Engage your senses to make the visualization more realistic. Take time here. Really see this picture.

Step into the Scene

- Imagine yourself stepping into this scenario. You are an active participant, not just an observer.
- See yourself in the situation, doing what you need to do to achieve your goal.

Embrace Emotions

- Feel the emotions associated with your success. If it's joy, confidence, love, or any other feeling, let it wash over you. Don't rush this part. We want the feeling to last even when the exercise is over.

Visualize Success

- Visualize the successful completion of your goal. Imagine the final steps and the sense of accomplishment. Note how that success feels for you. Sit with that feeling for some time.
- Notice who is there with you. Who are the people who will be happy and supportive? Who are the people who may not be? Just note it.

Overcome Challenges

- Visualize any challenges or obstacles that might come your way. What are they? See yourself successfully overcoming these challenges.

Maintain a Positive Mindset

- Throughout the visualization, maintain a positive and confident mindset. You believe in your ability to achieve this goal. If negative thoughts come into your head, gently set them aside and refocus on the positive.

Affirmations

- While visualizing, you can use affirmations or positive self-talk to reinforce your belief in your ability to achieve your goal.

End on a High Note

- As you conclude the visualization, see yourself celebrating your success and experiencing a profound sense of satisfaction. Take some time to note how great that profound sense of satisfaction feels.

Open Your Eyes

- When you're ready, open your eyes and return to the present moment.

Journal Your Experience

- Take a moment to capture the experience immediately after visualization. You can use these
  questions to prompt responses, or just have more
  of a free flow to the experience.
  - What specific emotions did you experience
    during this visioning exercise?
  - Can you identify any unexpected insights or
    new perspectives that emerged as you visu-
    alized your success and overcame potential
    obstacles?
  - In your mental imagery, did you notice any key
    strengths or resources within yourself that you
    can leverage to navigate challenges?
  - How did envisioning the completion of your
    goal make you feel?
  - Were there any moments during the exercise
    during which you found it challenging to main-
    tain focus? If so, what potential distractions or
    self-limiting beliefs did you observe?
  - As you pictured yourself in your desired out-
    come, did you notice any specific actions or
    behaviors that contributed to your success? If
    so, how can you incorporate them into your
    intentional actions moving forward?
  - In what ways has this visioning exercise clar-
    ified your intentions and empowered you to
    take deliberate actions towards your goals?

This visualization exercise is meant to be general and
adapted to all areas of your life. The key is to immerse

yourself in the mental image of your desired outcome and connect emotionally with the process to boost motivation to align your actions with your goals.

If you'd like more specific visualization exercises (for career, relationships, health, etc.), go to the website for some additional exercises.

Keep Visioning

Implementing a visualization practice into your routine helps keep the "impossible" in your sights—and start reaching it! The frequency of the visualization exercises you should engage in will vary depending on your goals, personal preference, and available time in your day. To be most effective, many experts recommend daily visualization exercises. Daily practice can help you enforce your goals and keep them at the forefront of your mind. It also helps you maintain a consistent and positive mindset. But, if that's too much for you (it may be, to start), consider implementing a weekly routine, or using visualization before engaging in activities that are related to your goals. For example, if you have an important meeting coming up, visualize it in detail beforehand to boost your confidence. If you're ever feeling stuck or demotivated, use it as a tool to rekindle your motivation and overcome mental blocks; we all have them, from time to time. You have the tool now to use as needed. Do it as often as you find beneficial for your specific goals and circumstances.

It's important to remember that the key to effective visualization is not just the frequency, but the *quality* of your practice. Your visualizations should be vivid, emotionally

What's something that seems so big to you that you have not allowed yourself to really consider it as a possibility? charged, and aligned with your values and desires. The more you practice, the more skilled you will become at creating compelling mental images and harnessing the power of visualization to help you achieve your goals.

Remember, I started this chapter with my "impossible."

What's something that seems so big to you that you have not allowed yourself to really consider it as a possibility?

Write it down, even if it seems it isn't realistic. In future visualization sessions, revisit these "impossible" goals and allow yourself to consider: what if it *is* possible?

Chapter 7

Creating Your Intentional Life

"Live with intention. Walk to the edge. Listen hard. Practice wellness. Play with abandon. Laugh. Choose with no regret. Do what you love. Live as if this is all there is."

– Mary Anne Radmacher

We're here! We're at the section of the book where we pull all the previous components together relating to where you are in your life to change your focus to where you want to *be*, and then give you the tools and resources to start doing the work to get you there. I'm so excited we're here!

This is, by design, a long chapter. If you've been able to fly through some of the previous chapters (I hope not), this is one that I hope you give yourself time to work through in multiple sittings, with *many* corresponding journal entries.

We'll start with some thought-provoking questions to get you thinking. The self-reflection questions you completed in Chapter Three asked you to assess where you are *now*. The point of these questions is to get you thinking more deeply about where you *want to go* and what your life will look like when you're there.

We'll then move on to defining your core values. You likely have them, but you'll work to put a name to them. As a defining North Star in our lives, representing who we are, this work requires us to know what values of ours will influence the life we want to build moving forward. We'll pull that together to make a personal mission statement.

Don't let me lose you here. I know, I know. I have worked in a big corporation, and the idea of mission statements, vision, and core values applied to my personal life would have me running for the hills. I acknowledge that hesitation if you have it, and empathize because I've been there, **but, trust me, this will help.** Only when you are very clear on your values, your life mission, and your priorities can you be intentional about how to get there. If you're still not convinced, humor me. We'll get there shortly.

Finally, I'll provide a list of activities that will become your toolbox for living intentionally every day. Making a habit of this process is what will keep you doing it regularly, coming back to it, and seeing the impact in your life.

But First, Some Questions

These questions may look familiar to you. A number of these were used in the "Self-Reflection" chapter to help you start thinking about your life *now*. These are focused on the *future* you're building.

These questions are meant to take you some time. **Don't rush this**. Grab your journal and your pen, find a comfy spot, break these questions into multiple journaling sessions, edit them, rewrite them, throw them out and write your own—just take the time to start reflecting about the life you want to build. These are here to help get the creative juices going, not to limit you. If these aren't the right questions for you, make them right.

- What do I want my relationship with my significant other to look like?
- What does the ideal relationship look like with my kids?
- What do I want my relationship to be with my nuclear and extended family?
- How do I want to nurture my most cherished relationships?
- What are my most important roles and responsibilities at this moment? (e.g. parent, employee, student, friend, partner)
- What does an ideal day look like for me?
- What things that are important to me do I want to accomplish in five years? Ten? Twenty?
- What do I want in my professional role?
- How do I want to feel about my profession?
- What's my ideal home environment look like?
- What are my physical goals?
- What's "balance" look like across areas of priority in my life in the future?
- Where do I feel the most content in my life right now? Do I envision that changing in any way? Where will I feel the most content and grateful?
- How do I want to nurture my mental well-being?
- What hobbies and leisure activities do I want to be involved in?

- How do I currently spend my time, and is it aligned with my goals and values?
- What are the daily habits and routines that shape my life right now, and are they serving me well?
- How do I want to spend my time daily? Weekly?
- What impact do I want to make in my community?
- What wider impact do I want to have in the world?
- What personal development goals do I want to accomplish?
- What do I want my financial situation to look like?
- What changes would I want to make to my current environment and living situation?
- What changes do I envision for my current main sources of stress and unhappiness in my life? What's it look like when I mitigate those?
- What brings me joy, fulfillment, and a sense of purpose?
- What aspects of my life do I feel the most content about and grateful for right now?
- What are the most significant challenges or obstacles I'm currently facing?

Your responses to these questions will serve for the goal setting that we'll do in an upcoming chapter. I included all of these questions in the chapter instead of putting most online so that you can continually come back here and ask yourself these questions over and over as you're building the life that you want to live.

Core Values: What They Are and Why They Matter

When I worked at a Fortune 500 company and I'd hear someone rattle on about mission, vision, and core values, I had to stifle a smirk because I didn't really think they meant much of anything. At least, not something *tangible* that I could see in my day-to-day life. Most likely unfairly, I would envision people in business suits sitting around a conference room, the walls adorned with posters extolling the virtues of "Teamwork!" and "Dreamwork!" With a whiteboard and a marker, they'd capture all the "corporate speak" that sounded good, but that was so vague it didn't mean anything at all to anyone in the room. It is not something into which I put any stock.

That is, until I started running my own company and someone said this comment that finally hit me: "Core values are what you hire for. It's what you fire for. It's who you *are*."

With that one sentence, I got it. I recognized that if you don't say what you stand for, if you don't share with the people who want to either join your team or are already on it what, as a company, matters to you, you can spend time with the wrong people, maybe not understanding why they're not the right fit. Something just feels off.

> "Core values are what you hire for. It's what you fire for. It's who you *are*."

And when I did that, it made hiring decisions much easier. It made performance conversations easier. It put words to something I innately *knew* but couldn't vocalize. So, I decided to do the same with my personal life, too. I recognized the value in putting a name to what I may have inherently thought about myself, and, in the process, I left with some surprises, too.

Take Sarah as an example. She was in a "fine" relationship, "fine" job, "fine" house. Everything was "fine." Until it wasn't.

When she started thinking about the core values that define her now and what she feels will be important to her in her life, she first wrote down "adventure." Then "family." So, because these resonated so much with who she is, it's no surprise that (as I shared earlier) she decided to travel alone for the first time and is still questioning whether she wants to be in a relationship that feels more like a roommate situation than a true partnership. She wants to *really* feel familial bonds with the person she intends to spend her life with, so, knowing how important that is to her, she's working through it and will decide where to go from here.

Core values are the fundamental principles and beliefs that guide your decisions, actions, and behaviors. They represent what's most important to you and reflect your deeply held convictions and priorities. They serve as a moral compass, influencing how you interact with others, the choices you make, and, overall, they help you take *action* when it comes to what's most important to you.

Ready to create yours?

Stop and Reflect

- **Set aside dedicated time.** Give yourself the time to work on this uninterrupted. Finding your core values is a thoughtful exercise that requires reflection. You don't want to be writing this list while standing at the kitchen counter, making dinner.
- **Start with a brainstorm.** Before reading past #2 (this one!), get out your journal and pen and begin by brainstorming a list of values that resonate with you. Write down anything that comes to mind, even if it seems trivial. If you need any inspiration, sneak a peek at the end of this chapter for some personal core values to get your creative juices flowing.

|Don't read further until you've created your list!|

- **Prioritize your list.** Of all the things you've written, what stands out most to you? Which of these values that you wrote down do you think have consistently guided your decisions and actions? If you had difficulty with brainstorming, now is the time to take a look at the end of the chapter, where I share some that you can consider. I didn't want you starting there, but as you are evaluating and identifying those on your list that feel authentic to you—which is our next step—I want you to have a full list to consider.
- **Identify authentic values.** Take a look at your list again. Are there any core values that you wrote down that feel like they are more influenced by

external pressure or societal expectations? If so, cross those off. Your core values are *yours* and should reflect your genuine beliefs and principles, not what you think they *should* include.

- **Use guiding questions.** If you're feeling stuck, ask yourself questions like:
  - o What values have consistently motivated my decisions and actions?
  - o What principles are most important to me in my relationships?
  - o When have I felt most fulfilled or content, and what values were present in those moments?
- **Consider scenarios.** What are some significant decisions or actions that you've taken in your life? What values were at the core of those decisions? In addition to "family" and "adventure," Sarah also included "growth" as a core value. She was feeling stagnant in her career. She wasn't learning new things in her role, and didn't feel like she was moving forward. She felt most of that was due to her direct supervisor, so she put changes in motion to move to another (more supportive) leader and team and hasn't looked back since.
- **Narrow down your list.** As you reflect and prioritize, aim to narrow down your list to a manageable number of core values—I recommend around three to five. I know it's hard to cut when so many things feel important to you. It's not to say that what doesn't make it to the list of core values isn't a priority in your life, but these are the three to five values that most profoundly influence your life choices.

Congrats on taking the first step in naming your core values! That wasn't too painful, was it? I didn't write "creating" your core values, because as you likely saw when working through this activity, they were always there. Now you have the words to use to define your guiding principles, and, in the next section, we'll work on creating a mission statement that details how you want to use those core values to live your authentic life.

Now that you're cognizant of what your values are, test them. Apply them to your everyday life and assess whether they feel right. Be open to change and adjust them as needed.

Finally, keep them visible. Print them out. Put them in your planner. Write them on your calendar. Doesn't matter. Just put them somewhere you will see them regularly. Seeing your list can help you be more intentional about making choices that are aligned with your core values. My book coach, Cathy, said that when she did this exercise, she put her core values at the top of her email inbox. When something came up, she could look at her core values to see if it was something she wanted to pursue or do, or not, based on its congruence with what mattered most to her. It led to her being more involved with volunteering in her community. Seeing it regularly was a daily reminder of what was most important to her.

Remember that the journey of identifying your core values is a highly personal one. There's no right

The key is to keep exploring, reflecting, and refining your core values over time, and to ensure that they resonate with your authentic self and guide your life choices.

or wrong way to do it, and you may find that your values evolve as you gain a deeper understanding of yourself by doing this work. The key is to keep exploring, reflecting, and refining your core values over time, and to ensure that they resonate with your authentic self and guide your life choices.

Writing a Personal Mission Statement

Now that you've identified three to five of your core values, consider crafting a personal mission statement that incorporates these values and outlines your purpose. We are still going to work through priorities across all areas of your life and the goals you have for each, so this is more of a high level exercise to put your core values into language and flesh them out a bit more beyond just three to five words.

For example, my core values are *authenticity*, *family*, *growth*, *balance*, and *contentment*.

I moved from my hometown for personal and professional development. I quit my corporate job to have freedom and flexibility in my schedule (seeking balance) so that I could prioritize my family. I'm seeking happiness and contentment every day with my commitment to living more intentionally.

So, I share my personal mission statement so you can use it as a template to bring your core values into yours.

Core Values: *Authenticity, Family, Growth, Balance, Contentment*

"My mission is to live an authentic life guided by the practice of intentionality, and the value of authenticity, which encourages me to be true to myself and others. I am committed to nurturing my family bonds and prioritizing the well-being of my loved ones. I actively seek personal growth, adventure, and lifelong learning, embracing change as an opportunity for self-improvement. I seek balance in all aspects of my life, fostering harmony between my career, family, and personal well-being. I aim to pursue happiness, contentment, and a positive outlook on life, finding joy in the little things every day."

Note that this mission statement doesn't bring in all of my goals and my priorities yet. We'll work on that next. Armed with your core values and your personal mission statement, we can then focus on the priorities that are most important to you across all areas of your life.

If you're feeling stuck in determining what three to five words sum up your core values, use the list below to generate ideas, and then use the example above as a reference for the mission statement with your words.

Core Values:

- **Adventure**: Embracing new experiences, exploration, and a dynamic sense of openness to life.
- **Authenticity:** Striving to be true to yourself and others; living in alignment with your beliefs and principles.

- **Balance:** Striving to maintain a harmonious and balanced life in various areas, such as work, family, and personal well-being.
- **Caring:** Showing care, concern, and affection for the people and causes that matter to you.
- **Community:** Contributing to the well-being and betterment of your local or global community through acts of kindness, service, or philanthropy.
- **Compassion:** Showing empathy and care for others, especially during times of need or suffering.
- **Connection to Nature:** Valuing and prioritizing a deep and respectful connection with the natural world, appreciating its beauty, diversity, and significance, and actively working to protect and preserve the environment for current and future generations.
- **Courage:** Facing challenges and adversity with bravery and determination.
- **Creativity:** Nurturing a creative spirit and seeking inspiration through making and interacting with arts.
- **Determination:** Demonstrating strong willpower and perseverance in pursuing goals.
- **Empathy:** Understanding and sharing the feelings of others and showing compassion.
- **Faith:** Cultivating a belief in a higher power and actively integrating spirituality into your life.
- **Family:** Placing a high value on the well-being and happiness of your family members and loved ones.
- **Forgiveness:** Letting go of grudges and resentment and offering forgiveness to others.
- **Flexibility:** Being adaptable and open to change in various life circumstances.

- **Gratitude:** Maintaining a sense of thankfulness and appreciating the positive aspects of life.
- **Growth:** Pursuing continuous personal development, self-improvement, and learning.
- **Honesty:** Upholding truthfulness and transparency in your actions and communications.
- **Inclusivity:** Embracing diversity and promoting equality and inclusivity in your interactions.
- **Independence:** Cherishing self-reliance and autonomy in personal decisions and actions.
- **Integrity:** Upholding a strong moral and ethical code, being honest, and doing what is right, even when no one is watching.
- **Joy:** Pursuing happiness, contentment, and a positive outlook on life; finding joy in the little things.
- **Justice:** Upholding fairness, equality, and the just treatment of all individuals, advocating for and contributing to systems that promote social justice and equity.
- **Kindness:** Acting with benevolence, generosity and consideration towards others.
- **Legacy:** Making a lasting and positive impact on the world, ensuring that your actions and contributions leave a meaningful legacy for future generations.
- **Mindfulness:** Practicing self-awareness, presence, and being in the moment.
- **Optimism:** Maintaining a positive outlook on life and focusing on solutions and opportunities.
- **Peace:** Cultivating a sense of inner tranquility and fostering harmony in relationships and communities, actively working towards conflict resolution and the well-being of all.

- **Respect:** Treating others with respect and valuing diversity and inclusivity in all interactions.
- **Serenity:** Striving for inner peace, calm, and a tranquil state of mind.
- **Service:** Committing to selfless acts of kindness, compassion, and support for others, dedicating time and resources to contribute positively to the welfare of the community and beyond.
- **Simplicity:** Embracing minimalism and decluttering to live a simpler, more meaningful life.
- **Well-Being:** Prioritizing physical and mental health and self-care to lead a fulfilling life.

This is a long list of core values that may apply to your personal life, but it is not exhaustive. Write ones that matter most to you.

Core values will vary based on your unique beliefs, experiences, and priorities. Defining your core values can provide a strong foundation for making intentional decisions and living a life that aligns with what matters most to you.

> Defining your core values can provide a strong foundation for creating the life you want to live.

In the next section, now that you're armed with your core values and personal mission statement, we will revisit your priorities and prioritize those values so you can start making time for what's most important to you.

Chapter 8

Prioritizing Your Priorities

*"The key is not to prioritize what's on your schedule,
but to schedule your priorities."*

– Stephen R. Covey

Isaiah can tell you that his wife is important to him. So is his daughter, Claire. So is his mom, and so are his two brothers and their families. His dad passed away last year. He has a job as an Enterprise sales manager for an educational learning company and is interested in advancing his career to the next step: a director role at the same firm. He travels as a part of his job, which he enjoys, but, sometimes, it can make fitting in his priorities feel like an impossible task. He gets to play golf a couple of times a month with his friends when he's in town—and on the occasional work trip. The nights he is traveling, he has gotten into the habit of going to the hotel lobby bar and eating a sandwich and fries for dinner, or pizza, having a couple of beers before going back into his hotel room to work a few more hours, catching up on emails sent when he was in meetings throughout the day. He isn't as physically fit as he used to be, but he has shrugged it off, attributing it to not having a standard routine and the reality that changes to his physical activity and diet are a lot harder when he is on the road.

He has never thought about intentionality. He instinctively knows what his priorities are, but hasn't thought about them any further than that.

But there is another way; a better way.

In this chapter, he'll get more granular about what his priorities mean to him, as will you.

In Chapter Three, you spent time coming up with your list of priorities in your life. You rated them, you sorted them into various buckets, and you created your master list of priorities that you will create time for while also setting goals for your future. And you posted them, right? Do you have them visible? If not, this is a good time to get them—I can wait. We're going to make those priorities much more specific, and then, in the next chapter, we're going to take those priorities and set some goals.

But first, let's explain the difference between the two. Goals and priorities are related concepts, but their nature and their influence on your actions are distinctly different. Since we'll be spending a lot of time on these two topics in this chapter, I'm going to make these differences crystal clear.

Priorities:

Priorities are aspects of your life that you consider to be the most important ones at a given time. Isaiah listed his wife, daughter, mom, extended family, and career. Think of the list you wrote earlier; perhaps it contained the names of family and friends, maybe you wrote about your physical and mental health. These are the things that you allocate your time, energy, and resources to first, because they are integral to achieving your objectives or living out your values.

They help with establishing a hierarchy of importance in your life. They help you decide where to focus your attention and effort. You may have multiple priorities, but you must decide which ones take precedence over others. Jaime's kids are both listed as priorities in her life, as is learning the piano. These are both important to her, but they obviously aren't weighted the same, and she allocates time for both of them based on that hierarchy.

Unlike goals, which are more time-bound, priorities may be more fluid and can change as circumstances in your life evolve. You may shift your priorities in response to changing needs or new opportunities. Before I met my Brazilian husband, learning Portuguese wasn't a priority in my life. Life evolved, and now it is. That's how it can shift. But if work is extremely demanding and I have to rank that priority higher for some time, I can do that. Priorities are more flexible.

Goals:

Goals are specific, measurable, achievable, relevant, and time-bound objectives that you aim to achieve. Some examples of goals are "obtain a professional certification in my field within the next twelve months" or "improve my cardiovascular fitness by running a 5k race in under thirty minutes within the next six months."

They're concrete targets that *align* with your priorities.

By design, goals have deadlines, giving you a sense of urgency that can help you stay on track to achieve them within a defined period.

Both priorities and goals are important for effective personal and professional planning, and for living your life more intentionally. We'll be spending time on both so you leave this chapter with more granular priorities, as well as some personal goals—and the tools to continue to develop them going forward.

Diving Deeper on Your Priorities

When Isaiah did the self-reflection exercise in Chapter Three, his priorities looked like this:

- *Kelly (his partner) - 5*
- *Claire (his daughter) - 5*
- *Career - 5*
- *Golf - 3, but main form of exercise, so don't want to eliminate it*
- *Faith - 5*
- *Career; working towards a promotion - 5*
- *Physical health; cut down drinking - 5*
- *Save more money for retirement - 5*
- *My mom (dad passed away) - 5*
- *Becoming more strategic about saving money (I want to go to Disney with my family) - 4*

When he wrote them out, he could see that his list wasn't very long and everything he wrote down was a top priority in his life. His faith, his relationship with his wife, his daughter, and his mom were all ranked at the top of the list, as was focusing on his career, in the interest of helping him take care of his family financially—and to surprise them with a trip. It doesn't feel like anything can be taken off this list; they're all important. There are a lot of things he thinks *should* be on his list, but he's unsure what to do about that. It's daunting enough when he looks at his list as is, because his typical day now feels strapped for time. How can he possibly make time for these priorities, much less any others?

We'll work on making time for priorities in the next chapter, but, first, we'll focus on getting much clearer on what making that priority a *priority* looks like for you.

Let's use Isaiah's list above as an example. I have copied that list below, but with added columns to help him start to think through what *specifically* he wants to start doing daily, weekly, monthly, or yearly to make each priority a *priority*. He struggled at first—and you might, too, because you're likely not used to thinking about the way you want to spend your time this granularly, or about how much time you want to spend on different priorities in your life. Isaiah worked through this exercise to come up with what focusing on that priority will look like for him. As I'll suggest to you in a moment, I asked him to start small. The goal isn't to write down *everything* that you want to do in these time periods for each priority, which would make this a stressful exercise, but just get the ideas flowing with one or two. Then, later, you can go back and add more when you get into the rhythm of thinking in this new way.

Note that these are not SMART goals (you'll learn about those more next chapter). We haven't tied metrics to these yet. These don't meet the definition of "goals." They are not intended to. This simply involves taking time to determine what it means to *you* for a priority to be a priority in your life.

Priority	Ranking	Daily	Weekly	Monthly	Yearly
Kelly	5	Coffee together before work.	I make dinner at least a couple nights a week.	Monthly date night.	Every other year, vacation together.
Claire	5	Thirty minutes of uninterrupted time just hanging out with her.	Pick her up at least once a week from school (miss this!)	**Come back to this; not sure.**	Family vacation at least every other year.
Job	5	Block schedule for at least two hours a day where I don't take meetings to get work done on my projects.	A coffee a week with someone from another team to network.	A coffee or meal with a member of the leadership team.	**I'm still thinking through this one.**
Golf	3	x	x	Golf - once/ month with friends.	x
Faith	5	Start and end the day with thanks/ gratitude.	Church with the family on Sunday.	x	x

Priority	Ranking	Daily	Weekly	Monthly	Yearly
Health - Lose some weight	3	Daily weigh in; cut back on drinking.	Watch what I eat, but treat day once a week.	Track progress every month.	x
Save more money for retirement	5	x	Need to set up call with financial advisor to adjust rates on pre-tax allocations.	x	x
Mom	5	Call or text daily	Longer call once a weekend.	Visit once per month.	Make sure she is at one of our houses for each of the holidays. Once a year we all (brothers) go to her house at the same time.
Saving for trip to Disney	3	Be mindful of spending; trying to save $2,000 by next year.	Track all weekly expenses.	See weekly expenses and after a month create a budget for different categories.	Disney!

Of all of the activities that you complete during your intentionality journey, you may find that *really* knowing what it looks like for you to make a particular priority a *priority* can have a demonstrable impact on and bring tremendous clarity to you on what matters most to you in your life.

Personally, I found that I needed to revisit what "my partner is a priority" meant to me, because I felt like, even though we were always around each other, our relationship was taking a back seat to other priorities. He has a full-time job; I own a market insights company and am writing a book; we have two kids in elementary school that we need to chauffeur to all of their activities; and we live in a city where we don't have family, so we need to ensure our plans include traveling out of town (and out of country) to get in the time we want to to focus on those relationships. We just have a *lot*—as we all do!—and I found that, without being intentional about what "my husband is a priority" really means to me, he wouldn't get my time: time that our relationship deserves. He would usually get the fall-down-tired-at-9 PM version of me after all the day's activities were over, after the dishes were done, the kitchen was cleaned up, and I could finally sit down and watch a show with him—where I would promptly fall asleep regardless of how scintillating the show was. I'll share examples in the next chapter about how to create time for your priorities, including your partner, but, first, I needed to get granular about how I wanted that priority to be represented in my life. So what did "Otavio—my husband—as a priority" mean to me? How did I want to make time for us daily? Weekly? Monthly? Yearly?

More importantly, what do your priorities look like when you're a lot more granular about what they are?

Your turn.

It's your turn to start thinking, with more specificity, about what you want that priority to look like daily, weekly, monthly, yearly.

Here's how:

- Set aside dedicated time to self-reflect. As best as you can, find a place in the house, in a park, in your yard, or anywhere where you can be alone with your thoughts for a set amount of time.
- Either create a grid like the one above in your journal or go to the website to print out a worksheet to fill in.
- Write in all of the priorities that you listed from Chapter Three, "Self Reflection: Starting the Work," on the left hand side of the table.
- Come up with one to two ideas about how you want that priority to be represented in your life. You may have some priorities that don't warrant time spent on them daily; no problem. Especially if, unlike Isaiah, your list includes some priorities that are much lower than a five. Write them all down, though. You may not need to make time for them daily, but you want them on your radar.

Stop and Reflect

1. What, if anything, surprised you when doing this exercise?
2. How can being more granular about the time you want to make for each of your priorities help you?
3. How will you hold yourself accountable to the time that you've indicated you want to create for each of these priorities?

Now that you've gotten more granular about your priorities and you've thought through what making that priority a priority means to you daily, weekly, monthly, yearly, etc., in the next chapter, we'll talk about creating specific goals around your priorities, how to find time to hit those goals, and how not to lose them and all the work you did here. How do you keep it all top of mind? Read on! :)

Chapter 9

Setting Goals

*"The tragedy in life doesn't lie in not reaching your goal.
The tragedy lies in having no goals to reach."*

— Benjamin Mays

Katie worked in a product management position in a technology company for years. She was good at her job. It wasn't her passion, but it paid the bills and she liked her team. Time passed until one day, she realized, "Holy crap! I've been here for two decades! How is that even possible?"

It's amazing how it can just sneak up on you like that, isn't it? She was single, living in San Francisco. She had a great group of friends, she played in a band. Life was good.

But she wasn't *completely* content. She had been doing the equivalent of swiping right on countless versions of dating apps over the years, but she hadn't found a person who was as badass as she is (my explanation, not hers). She knew she wanted a family, but she just wasn't finding a partner that met her criteria, so she set a goal. She would start a family by the time she was forty-five years old, regardless of how she made it happen. She wrote it down, she put plans in place, and, a couple of years later, she became a single mother by choice, meeting an incredible group of other women by sharing her experience via a personal blog.

A few years and two children later, she decided it was time to make a longtime dream of hers a reality. While working her day job and taking care of her children, she put another goal in place. She was going to start her own business. She wrote it down, gave herself a deadline, took classes in the evenings to sharpen her skills, and, now, is the successful owner of a digital marketing company that works with small businesses to best tell their story.

She's an inspiration not just for me, but for many other people, and I share her story here because her goals were *lofty.* Have children on your own? Leave twenty years of security and start your own business? With two small kids? Move across the country, while you're at it? It's a tremendously brave step and she's crushing it in both areas now in her new city.

> These types of big achievements don't happen on their own, and they don't happen without planning.

I know her personally, so there's a lot of things I could attribute this to, but the one that resonates with me and is why I share this vignette in this chapter is this—she was **specific about the goals that she wanted to accomplish.** These types of big achievements don't happen on their own, and they don't happen without planning. That's why we're going to spend some time now working on yours.

Why Set Goals?

In the last chapter, you worked on prioritizing your priorities. But, as I discussed, there's a key difference between priorities and goals. While priorities are the broad, overarching areas of importance in your life that guide your decision-making, goals are the specific, time-bound targets that provide the **actionable steps to realize our priorities.**

You know I love to start with the "why." Here are reasons it's worth setting personal goals:

- **Clarity and Direction:** Personal goals provide you with clarity about what you want to achieve in life. They help you define your aspirations, dreams, and the directions you want to take. Katie wanted to be a mom, so she made it happen. First, she needed to be clear that this was a priority. I love how she explained this to me: "One of the ways I knew this was a priority, other than every cell in my body screaming it, was that, whenever I got onto a path that moved away from it (dating someone who didn't want kids, for example), I got depressed. That's the 'body compass' putting me on my path."
- **Motivation:** Goals act as powerful motivators. When you set specific objectives, you're more likely to be enthusiastic and committed to taking action to achieve them. Isaiah was motivated to take his family on a big family vacation to Disney. Thinking about what the experience would be like for his kids kept him on track and motivated when it was tough to save the money weekly.

- **Focus:** Being specific about your goals helps you focus your time, energy, and resources on what truly matters to you. It enables you to prioritize tasks and activities that align with your objectives.
- **Measurable Progress:** Goals allow you to measure your progress and success. They provide a sense of achievement as you make strides toward your desired outcomes. Personally, I review my goals every week to see how I'm tracking towards them, and it's this personal accountability that keeps me on track.
- **Personal Growth:** Pursuing goals often involves personal development. You acquire new skills, knowledge, and experiences as you work toward your objective. Take Jaime for example, who decided that learning Spanish was a priority for her. Once she got outside of her comfort zone and allowed herself to be a complete novice in an area again, she found that it opened her up to considering other things she wanted to learn.
- **Increased Resilience:** Having goals can enhance your resilience. When faced with challenges or setbacks, you're more likely to persevere and find alternative solutions to reach your goals. In Isaiah's goal to lose some weight, he decided to implement a weight tracking app into his daily routine. If he saw his weight go up on a given day, or if he got off track during one of his business meetings, when staying on his plan was difficult, he was encouraged that it was just one day and knew he could get back on track easily the next.

- **Enhanced Well-Being:** Achieving your goals can lead to a sense of fulfillment and well-being. It boosts your self-esteem and self-confidence. Who has given themselves a goal, worked towards it, and then hit it? If you have, you know how good that can feel!
- **Time Management:** Goals can improve your time management skills as you allocate your time more efficiently to tasks that contribute to your objectives. You become more adept at removing distractions and at not focusing on things that aren't important to you while making time for what is.
- **Life Satisfaction:** Goal achievement is linked to greater life satisfaction. When you work toward meaningful goals, you're more likely to feel content and fulfilled. This is my hope for everyone reading this book. It's that, by living more intentionally, by setting goals, by achieving them, you feel the contentment and satisfaction that it brings to your life.
- **Freedom:** Setting and achieving goals gives you a sense of control over your life. *You* choose. You decide what's important to you. You decide where you spend your time. You decide what's *worth* your time. You decide what's important to you. It's empowering when you realize the control that you have over your life.

Sold on the importance of setting goals yet?

If you want to be on the path to making more intentional choices, staying motivated, and reaching your dreams, setting goals is absolutely fundamental to personal development and living a purpose-driven life.

Now that we know *why* setting goals is so important, let's get into *how* to set them.

Creating Your Goals

There are various methodologies and frameworks for goal setting that can help you state your goals clearly and keep yourself on track. In this chapter, we'll focus on a simple framework to help create goals that are well-defined, actionable, and effective.

SMART goals.

SMART stands for:

- Specific
- Measurable
- Actionable
- Relevant
- Time-Bound

This goal-setting theory emerged from the work of management scholar Peter Drucker in the 1950s. It was then further developed and popularized by George T. Doran in a 1981 paper titled "There's a S.M.A.R.T Way to Write Management's Goals and Objectives," which was published in *Management Review.* From there, it gained widespread recognition for its ability to help with the creation of clear and attainable objectives across various areas.

There's one caveat here. No one goal setting technique is the be-all and end-all approach, with no contest between experts on their effectiveness. For that reason, I'll provide some other framework examples for you to consider. What's most important to me in this book is not to showcase empirical evidence of the effectiveness of one goal setting framework over another, but to share with you what has worked for me personally and to give you options to consider. The most important facet of the chapter is this: Write down your goals and track your progress. The framework you decide to use will be the one that works best for you, or is a mix of some of the ones below.

> The most important facet of the chapter is this: Write down your goals and track your progress.

Understanding SMART Goals:

- **Specific:** Goals are detailed and precise, leaving no room for ambiguity. They target a specific area for improvement. For example, "improve fitness" is vague. "Run a 5k" is more specific.
- **Measurable:** These goals include criteria for measuring progress. Quantifiable metrics are used to track achievement. For example, "save $5,000 for down payment on house within twelve months" is measurable, allowing you to track your savings against the target.

- **Achievable:** SMART goals are realistic and feasible, within your abilities and resources to achieve. I'm not going to write "launch my first album by the end of the year" when I don't have an agent, don't play a musical instrument, and am a questionable karaoke performer at best. It's not realistic.
- **Relevant:** Goals need to align with your values, aspirations, and broader objectives. To return to the example above, it wasn't achievable, nor was it relevant to my life. Relevant goals for a business owner, as I am, may be something more along the lines of "attend one networking event per month for the next quarter," if my aim is to continue to grow my business.
- **Time-Bound:** Setting a deadline gives your goal urgency and focus. A time-bound goal would be "write a fifty page e-book on personal finance within three months."

On the topic of time-bound, how much time should you allocate to hitting your goals?

I recommend ninety days. I've read a lot of research that supports setting short-term, mid-term, and long-term goals, but for the purposes of this book, I'm suggesting starting with a ninety-day goal-setting cadence. Why?

- **You can accomplish something *meaningful* in ninety days.** Achieving short-term goals creates a sense of momentum and motivation. You can accomplish something big in ninety days. Ninety days strikes a balance between being short enough to help you to maintain focus, while being long enough to achieve significant milestones, enabling you to track your progress effectively. Hitting your goals often leads to increased confidence in the process, so the likelihood to pursue subsequent goals increases.

- **You start working on your goals *now*.** If you have a big, lofty goal that's "out there," meaning a year or two in the future, you can procrastinate. You likely *will* procrastinate. "Out there" goals don't require you to start making changes now to hit them. A shorter timeframe helps improve focus and commitment. It doesn't allow you to wait. You can clearly envision the steps needed to achieve your goals when the goal post isn't too far into the future.

- **You can focus and commit.** If you're working to accomplish meaningful goals in ninety days, you can't overcommit. You can't list ten meaningful goals you want to hit *and* actually hit them all. So, you are forced to commit. What are the three or four goals you'll *commit* to hitting in this timeframe? By being clear on what those goals are, as well as about the timeframe in which you'll hit them, you're more likely to feel committed to them.

Remember what we discussed in Chapter Six, "Visioning Change." Don't let the idea of ninety days make you feel limited in pursuing big goals. I gave an example from my experience in that chapter, that I never could have imagined being able to live and work in another country with the job that I had. It was too big, too out there. But it was something I knew I wanted to be able to do *some time, somehow.* It took a while to get from visioning that other reality to that reality actually happening, so "leaving my company to be able to live in another country for a month out of the year" is not a goal. However, I could break down that big vision into smaller, attainable, time-bound goals.

Here's an example. If your vision is "I want to start my own interior design business someday," that's what you envision doing "sometime." It's not a goal. It's a vision of how you want your life to look differently down the road. What you *can* do is break this into goals to start making meaningful movement on fulfilling that bigger dream. Your ninety-day goals may look more like this:

- "I will take an online course about opening up a small business by (end date ninety days out)."
- "I will save an additional 10% of every paycheck for the next three months to build an emergency fund when I start my business (and keep this as a goal every quarter until you launch)."
- "I will create my LinkedIn profile and post three times a week through (end date ninety days out) to start building my brand in interior design."

All of these goals would help you realize that bigger vision of starting your own interior design company in small, measurable, attainable, relevant, and time-bound steps.

Your turn.

In this section, you'll create three to four goals that you'll commit to for the next ninety days. This worksheet, which you can also find online, will help you think through your goal in more detail before you write it down. You can download a sheet on the website.

SMART Goal Worksheet

Goal Title: _____

Specific: What exactly do you want to accomplish? Be clear and detailed.

- What is the goal you want to achieve?
- Who is involved?
- What resources or constraints are there?
- Where will this goal take place?
- Why is this goal important to you?

Measurable: How will you know when the goal is achieved?

- What metrics or criteria will you use to track progress?
- How will you measure your success?
- What milestones will you use to track your progress?

Achievable: Is the goal realistic and attainable considering your resources and abilities?

- What steps or actions are necessary to achieve this goal?
- Do you have the skills, knowledge, and resources required?
- Is the goal within your reach, or does it require additional support or learning?

Relevant: Is this goal meaningful and aligned with your values, aspirations, or broader objectives?

- How does this goal align with your personal or professional objectives?
- Why is this goal important to you and your growth?
- How will achieving this goal contribute to your larger vision?

Time-Bound: When will you achieve this goal? Set a specific timeframe.

- What is the deadline for accomplishing this goal?
- Are there any smaller deadlines or milestones along the way?
- How will you manage your time to ensure progress?

1. Complete this exercise for each of your goals.
2. With your worksheet in hand, now craft your three to four SMART goals, making each goal one sentence.
3. Use this checklist to ensure your goals are SMART.

SMART Goal Checklist

Goal: _____

Specific:

- Is the goal well-defined and clear?
- Does it answer the questions *who*, *what*, *when*, *where*, and *why*?
- Can someone else understand exactly what you want to achieve?

Measurable:

- Have you established criteria for measuring progress?
- Is there a way to quantify or track your success?
- Are there specific metrics or milestones to indicate progress?

Achievable:

- Is the goal realistic and within your capabilities?
- Have you broken down larger goals into smaller, more manageable steps?
- Do you have the necessary resources—or access to them—to achieve this goal?

Relevant:

- Does the goal align with your priorities and values?
- Is this goal important for your personal or professional growth?
- Will achieving this goal contribute meaningfully to your larger vision?

Time-Bound:

- Have you set a specific deadline or timeframe for achieving the goal?
- Are there smaller deadlines or milestones along the way?
- Is the timeframe realistic and conducive to making progress?

Use this checklist as a guide to ensure that your goals meet the criteria of being **Specific**, **Measurable**, **Achievable**, **Relevant**, and **Time-Bound**. Reviewing your goals using these criteria can help refine and strengthen them, setting you on a clear path towards successful goal attainment.

Other Approaches

I started this chapter by stating that SMART is a popular framework for goal-setting, but it is not the only one. If goal-setting is new to you, though, especially for personal development, I recommend starting with one and getting the hang of writing down your goals, reviewing them regularly, and then holding yourself accountable at the end of the ninety-day mark. Did you hit them? If no, why not? Was the goal unattainable in that timeframe? Did external influences have an impact? If so, what were they, and how can you effectively address them next time? Get into the goal-setting and review its flow before making too many tweaks. However, if you find that SMART goals, for whatever reason, aren't the right fit for you, there are other models to consider. You can find worksheets online to download if you want to try out any of these approaches.

OKRs (Objectives and Key Results):

OKRs are a goal-setting framework popularized by companies like Google. I first read about them in the book *Measure What Matters* by John Doerr, and we follow this goal-setting approach at my company. This approach involves setting ambitious *objectives*—what you want to achieve—and defining *key results*—specific and measurable outcomes that indicate success. OKRs encourage aspirational goals and measurable outcomes, as well as fostering alignment and focus across teams or personal endeavors.

BHAGs (Big, Hairy, Audacious Goals):

Coined by business author Jim Collins, BHAGs are ambitious and visionary goals that go beyond a person's immediate capabilities but inspire motivation and innovation. These are "think big" goals that have a transformative impact and align with your long-term vision.

Backward Goal Setting:

This technique involves visualizing the end goal and then working backward to determine the steps needed to achieve it. By starting with the end in mind, you can create a clear roadmap for reaching your desired outcome.

Scrum (or Agile) Goal Setting:

Adapted from software development, Scrum or Agile methodologies involve breaking larger goals into smaller, more manageable tasks or sprints. It emphasizes flexibility, adaptability, and iterative progress, allowing for adjustments based on feedback.

Personal Development Plans:

These plans involve a holistic approach to goal setting, encompassing personal and professional growth. They include elements such as skill development, education, health, relationships, and career aspirations, allowing for a comprehensive self-improvement strategy.

Habit Stacking:

Rather than setting specific goals, habit stacking focuses on creating routines and habits that lead to desired outcomes. By linking new habits to existing ones, you gradually build a chain of behaviors that support your objectives.

The most important part of goal setting isn't the framework you use. The ninety day timeline in a SMART format works best for me, so I share it here in more detail. Use these tools (or search for others) to explore other approaches that suit your preferences, personality, and objectives. While SMART goals provide structure, these methods offer additional direction and flexibility in achieving your personal and professional milestones. I have no idea what tool, specifically, Katie used to make her big vision dream a reality, but I know that she wrote them down, reviewed them regularly, and held herself accountable. Keep that in mind. The tool you use is less important than the process of writing your goals down, reviewing them regularly and tracking your progress, and ultimately, holding yourself accountable to them at the end of the ninety days.

> The tool you use is less important than the process of writing your goals down, reviewing them regularly and tracking your progress, and ultimately, holding yourself accountable to them at the end of the ninety days.

You're thinking big, you defined your priorities, you prioritized them, you set goals. Now, let's discuss how to create time to meet your goals.

Chapter 10

Creating Time

*"The way we spend our days becomes our weeks, becomes our months, becomes our years, becomes our **life**. Plan wisely."*

– Gina Boedeker

"I don't have time to exercise."
"I don't have any time for myself."
"I don't have time to see my friends."
"I don't have time for… (fill in the blank)."

What do you tell yourself? What are you saying you don't have time for?

Grab your pen, grab your journal, and <u>don't skip this part.</u>

What don't you feel like you have time for?

1. _____
2. _____
3. _____
4. _____
5. _____

Don't feel limited by these five lines. Keep going. If you feel like you don't have time for things that are important to you, for the priorities that you've listed in previous exercises, capture them all now.

Because the goal of this chapter is to help you find the time and to change this.

Remember Jane from the introduction to this book? She's the hospital administrator that was waking up tired every day, running around to get kids to their events, going to meetings all day, and feeling fall-down tired at the end of the day.

Where in the heck is there time in her schedule?

If your day is similar, where in the heck is there time in *your* day?

In this chapter, we're going to go over how to *create* time in your day. The time is there. We all have the same twenty-four hours in the day, but how we choose to *structure* our day can have a profound impact on us not only feeling like we have the ability, but actually fitting in our top priorities. I'll provide a number of techniques I've implemented in my own life and give you ample opportunities to pause and reflect on how implementing these strategies could help you create the day you want. Because, reiterating the quote from the start of this chapter, how we spend our days becomes how we spend our weeks, becomes how we spend our months, becomes how we spend our years, becomes how we spend our *lives*. What could be more important than that?

This section is important. Create the time to allow yourself to absorb this.

Creating Time Strategies

Weekly Planning

Find a day in your week to consistently plan out what the following week will look like. Look to your priorities list and make sure that you have time allocated based on what *you* decided that priority should look like. Keep in mind that there are weeks you may not be able to fit it all in, even with the best of planning. That's okay. The important piece here is that you're intentional about what you have allocated time to in your priorities—and what you want to make time for.

I do this activity every Friday afternoon before I close out my week. I will look to the following week to make sure I've made time for:

- Drop-offs and pickups from school, with hard stops in my schedule as needed
- Time to exercise, at least four to five times a week
- Time out in nature
- Time with my kids
- Time with my husband
- Meetings for work
- Deep work and big picture thinking for work-life
- Business development

Stop and Reflect

1. Revisit the priorities that you've written out.
2. Pull up the calendar that you'll use for personal and professional priorities.

3. Write out the meetings and appointments that are already in your calendar for next week.
4. After you read through the rest of the strategies below, you'll come back to your calendar and fill it in with more detail. Keep it handy. You're about to have next week planned out.

If you would like a template for weekly planning around your priorities, go to the website.

Time Blocking

Time blocking is dedicating blocks of time to specific tasks or activities. It allows you to focus your attention on a singular task during a defined timeframe, diminishing distractions, enhancing your productivity, and making sure you have the time allotted to get done what needs to be done.

You simply cannot give the best of yourself to anyone else, or to any other priorities, if you aren't making time for yourself to be physically and mentally well.

What goes into time blocking? Here's the beauty of this—*you* get to decide. Here are some things you may want to start blocking time for in your schedule, which, naturally, will depend on the type of work that you do and the priorities that are most important to you. I'll use some of the examples above and go a bit deeper to show how they're blocked. The goal here is to just get you brainstorming.

- **Deep work.** A major change Jane made to her schedule was to start blocking out time every week to think about higher level goals and initiatives that usually get put on the backburner with all of the meetings that typically take up her time. Strategy? Deep thinking sessions? Who in the heck had time for that? She didn't. Most of us don't. Until we decide to change it, block the time, and *honor* it as we would any other meeting on our calendar.

- **Project work.** Hitting client deadlines is a critical component of many jobs, and teams can struggle with being able to make time to do "actual work" when there are other demands on their calendar. Have you experienced this in your role? Is it possible for you to block time on your calendar for specific projects during specific times in your day, and for you to treat that time block as a commitment to yourself to do the work you know you need to do in that time? That way, if someone asks you, "Are you free Monday at noon?" you can reply, "No, sorry. Can we shoot for (insert date/time)?" These are the commitments that tend to get broken when other people request your time. Try to be disciplined about using the time you block out for the task, as you know what you need to get done and when you need to do it.

- **Commuting.** We don't always think about commuting as time we have available in our schedule. How often do we see the traffic starting up and get physically uncomfortable, knowing how much longer it will take us to get to where we want to go?

Block out the time; know the time that it takes to get from point A to point B and *plan* out how you want to spend that time. Audio book you want to listen to? Podcast? Take it a step further and plan out exactly what you want to accomplish during that time. When stuck in traffic, Jaime has some go-to podcasts for Spanish, spending the time doing something that gets her further in accomplishing one of her priorities. There is a lot of time in this window for some of us; plan to make good use of it.

- **Exercise.** Finding an hour in our schedules doesn't magically happen. We have to block the time and plan our day around it. In speaking with many people about how they can fit all they need to into their schedules, this is the goal that is easily tossed. It shouldn't be. It can't be. I am drawn to the quote, "if you don't make time for your wellness, you'll be forced to make time for your illness." You simply cannot give the best of yourself to anyone else, or to any other priorities, if you aren't making time for yourself to be physically and mentally well. Make the time by blocking the time.

- **"Coffees."** In this context, I don't necessarily mean meeting someone at a coffee shop, but sometimes it's that. Block time for networking, for having catch-ups with friends, with family, with people you want to meet. If you work in a remote environment, you may miss out on those casual "hey, wanna get a coffee?" moments in the day. Plan for them. Invite people to have a coffee and do so virtually to catch up.

- **Time with your partner.** If you wrote in the previous sections that making time for your partner or spouse is a priority, the time won't simply open up without you planning for it. It's easy for priorities involving work and kids to easily take over that time. Consider blocking out part of your calendar at any time in the day when you can have uninterrupted time together. Even if it's only ten minutes to reconnect, it's time. If working remotely, are you saving time on a commute, on not getting that coffee with colleagues? Can you take thirty minutes to have a coffee with your partner? Are there shared activities that you can do together, or as a family? Can you make time in your week for a walk?

- **Dating.** If you're not in a relationship but want to be, blocking time to engage in online dating platforms is an activity a good friend of mine said he needs to do in order to "make" himself stay on top of what he said sometimes feels like a lot of work. Instead of the constant interruptions and distractions throughout the day, he plans on checking new connections when he gets home from work, and it's become a routine that feels more manageable than trying to make time for it throughout the full day.

- **Family priorities.** What are the times that you absolutely want to have with your family on a regular basis? Do you schedule it? Katie is a single mom, and having the flexibility to drop her kids off and pick them up from school every day has been a priority for her since they went to school. So, she makes sure she blocks out time in her calendar for drops-offs and pick-ups. It doesn't mean she doesn't work before and after that time, but she pauses work to get that time in with them most days out of the week, unless something is pressing. Your priority may not be drop-offs or pick-ups. Maybe it's your kids' sporting activity, or play, or concert, or (fill-in-the-blank). Whatever is important to you to show up the way you want to, plan it out by blocking the time in advance, so people know you're not available at that time.

- **Meal prepping.** The weeks when I am able to get out ahead of planning my meals and knocking out a few all at one time are the weeks I say to myself, "Why don't you do this all the time?" It allows me to make healthy meals in a block of time on Sundays, while listening to an audio book, in the flow, and then I put them in the refrigerator for when we're ready to eat them. It saves a lot of time *and* mental energy for me throughout the week.

Stop and Reflect

1. Make a list of the time blocking methods mentioned above that would be the most helpful for you to implement.
2. Brainstorm additional activities and priorities you could time block that are not listed above.
3. Pull up your calendar for next week and *start*. Plan out how you'd like to approach your day or your week and block off time in your schedule for specific tasks.

Fitting It All In – 16:8 Method

We lament that there are simply not enough hours in the day to get everything done that we need to for our work, at home, for ourselves, our families. I know, it's a real challenge.

The Bureau of Labor and Statistics stated that the typical American worker works 8.8 hours a day. Add onto that commuting time, where the latest Census data showed an average commute time of 27.6 minutes one way (likely down more now due to more work from home scenarios post COVID), and that 8.8 hours jumps up to closer to **9.5 hours per day** for a lot of U.S. workers to get to work, to get home from work, and actually *work*.

The expectation of an 8 hour (plus) work day is likely not changing anytime soon. It's pervasive. What started out as a campaign during the Industrial Revolution by workers whose over twelve- to sixteen-hour days were helping factories optimize outputs led to a successful campaign to reduce hours across many industries. In fact, in 1914 Henry Ford was the first CEO to implement the eight-hour work day as a standard for his employees. It's a practice that has stuck and is the unwritten expectation now for full-time jobs.

So, our time is blocked for work. We know this. It's a requirement. It's planned out. It's rigid. Usually, it's a chunk of our time where only work happens. I have found that rigidity, for me, made meeting expectations on *other* priorities or attaining goals outside of work difficult. They got put on the backburner.

This continued until I implemented an important change, and I only did *that* when I came to this realization: **I was not planning out most of my day.** Twenty-four hours in a day, and I was "loose" with all the other time outside of my standard work hours.

Based on countless conversations with people about intentionality and creating more time in their day, I learned that this was the norm. *Most* people are not planning out their day in detail outside of work hours. The most common responses that I received were that people treat their work and personal calendars differently. Their work calendars are primarily filled up with meetings that other people set for them and rarely include all the tasks that they need to accomplish (which are more commonly tracked on to-do lists for the day). On the personal front, it was most common to hear that there's a family calendar with appointments throughout the month visible in a shared location, but the two calendars rarely overlap, unless it's for appointments outside of standard work hours (i.e. client dinners or early starts that would impact the full family).

> The *only* way that I have found I can get in everything that I want to—and need to—is more effectively planning out my *full* day.

Work obligations on one calendar with meetings. Personal calendar displayed for the family at another location.

I had to make a change. That approach was no longer working for me. The *only* way that I have found I can get in everything that I want to—and need to—is more effectively planning out my *full* day. I call it using the 16:8 method. The 16:8 method means planning out sixteen hours of a twenty-four-hour day, and planning eight hours of sleep per night. For me, specifically, I have a schedule from 6:00 AM - 10:00 PM *most* days (no, I'm not a robot, and yes, there's room for spontaneity—more on this below).

This means I have had to pull back from the 9:00 - 5:00 mentality for work, and I can tell you, after over fifteen years of working in a corporate position and then holding myself to that same rigid schedule for years, when I started my company, this has been a very difficult habit to break.

I used to equate doing my job effectively to *also* being at my desk during the standard work hours. But when I planned work only during those times (other than the occasional client dinner or breakfast, or team meetings outside those standard hours), I struggled to fit in what I needed to in all areas of my life.

I have a caveat here. This may not work for everyone, and may not work for every industry. I recognize that I created this after working in a corporate position (where it would work) and now use it regularly in a service-based business, where my team must hit client deadlines, but have some flexibility of when and where this work can be done. Not every industry works this way. A bartender can't run errands during his shift. A pilot isn't micromanaging personal priorities while flying a plane. If this doesn't work for you *exactly*, think about the pieces of it that resonate with you that could be implemented.

Also, I recognize that not every company and not every manager is going to be supportive of the 16:8 method at first, even if they're at companies where this could be really effective. They likely haven't heard of it, don't understand it, don't see why it's helpful, and may be fearful that you'll pull back from deadlines or work priorities. It's a natural first reaction, though it's one I will cover how to overcome in the following chapter about how to get buy-in on your priorities from your manager and team.

I recognize that having my own company affords me a bit more flexibility to implement this method and schedule my time the way that I want to, so it may be easy to say, "It's her company, she can do it!" But I also know my *whole team* has this type of flexibility to schedule their day to fit in their personal priorities that they need to attend to during the typical work day hours. We have built a culture of ownership, trust, and professionalism, so they know they can be trusted to not have "butts in seats" for every minute of their eight hours in a nine-to-five typical workday, and I know that they'll work outside their typical workday hours to make up time if needed or to accomplish what needs to be done for our clients. I run a business. Our deliverables can't decrease because of this approach—I'd go so far as to say they're *better* because of our approach.

Those caveats aside, here's a real example of what the 16:8 method looks like for me:

6 AM - Wake up; write (goal today: finish this chapter in Hard Stop)

6:30 AM - (blocked from 6-7:30)

7:00 AM - (continued blocked from 6-7:30)

7:30 AM - Wake up kids, get them ready for school, get ready for work

8:00 AM - Breakfast

8:30 AM - Drop kids at school

9:00 AM - Read/reply to emails

9:30 AM - Team huddle

9:45 (9:45 - 10:30) AM - work on proposal

10:00 AM- Proposal

10:30 AM - Work on marketing strategy document through 11:30

11:00 AM - strategy document
11:30 AM - strategy document
12:00 PM - Eat lunch; hike through 1:30 (continue on marketing strategy during hike**)
12:30 PM -
1:00 PM (1:15 arrive back, quick shower)
1:30 PM - 15 minute sales meetings 1:30, 1:45, 2:00, 2:15, 2:30, 2:45, 3:00
2:00 PM - sales
2:30 PM - sales
3:00 PM - Reply to emails, and put all notes into CRM
3:30 PM - Pickup kids from school
4:00 PM - Write blog posts, marketing content for LI (block for hour)
4:30 PM - Continued; write out schedule for tomorrow
5:00 PM - Luiz haircut (bring book to read)
5:30 PM -
6:00 PM - cook dinner (hang out with Otavio and kids)
6:30 PM -
7:00 PM - dinner
7:30 PM - clean up dinner, get organized for tomorrow
8:00 PM - Simpsons with fam
8:30 PM - Kids in bed
9:00 PM - read
9:30 PM - read/sleep

A couple of things I want to call out here. I didn't stop working when I went on a hike. I was out in nature, I was exercising, but I *also* had a pile of small index cards with some topics written out that I wanted to work through. Instead of sitting at my desk, I thought about them and worked on them while walking. I use the voice recorder on my iPhone, and I also just email myself "hiking notes" that I add to while I'm walking.

You can be intentional not *only* about being out and getting exercise, but about what you want to focus on during that time.

Do you feel like you just need an escape and you don't want to purposefully think about anything big? Do you have work or personal questions you're working through and want to focus your thoughts on those while exercising? Do you want to just feel more meditative and reflective while exercising? Do you want to escape for a bit and listen to a podcast, audiobook, or music?

Your turn.

Go to your journal and plan out what your 16:8 looks like, using start and end times for your day that fit your schedule. Not everyone wants to start planning at 6 AM, and not everyone (myself included) can stay awake past midnight anymore. Here's how to start:

- Either write out your start and end times in your journal, or go to the website to get customizable templates that you can fill in.
- Start by planning out your day tomorrow.
- Refer to the priorities you've already listed out and start time blocking your day, overlaying (if and when possible) your work and personal priorities into your full day.
- If you commute, plan out what you want to do during that commute. It's okay if you want to listen to sports radio and veg out; that's entertainment, and if it's important to you, that's worth making time for. But if you want to make use of the time another way, be mindful about that.

- Plan your full sixteen hours and give yourself ample time to sleep.
- Do this for a few more days this week and see if your weekly priorities are making it into your weekly plan.

Stop and Reflect

1. What couldn't you make time for?
2. How did planning out the full day allow you to fit more into it?
3. What challenges might you have with combining personal and professional schedules into one?
4. How do you think this approach would be received by your managers or leadership team if you need to take care of some personal priorities during the typical work hours (if you'll be making up the time/ responsibilities outside of those standard work hours)?

Time Boxing

Time boxing is breaking work into intervals of concentrated effort followed by short breaks. Why do this? It helps boost productivity by combating burnout, sustaining energy levels, and improving concentration through periodic, restorative breaks. And let's be honest. How long can you focus on something without losing concentration? How long is your attention span? Research on this topic varies. An article published by Harvard Health Publishing in 2020 stated that the amount of concentration time will vary by person, and ranges from ten to fifty-two minutes.

I'm a big fan of the Pomodoro method. Developed by Francesco Cirillo in the 1980s, it's a time management method that utilizes a kitchen timer to break work into twenty-five minute intervals. At the end of the interval, you take a short break. The name comes from the Italian word for "tomato," after the tomato-shaped kitchen timer Cirillo used when he was a student.

The idea is simple, but powerful.

- Determine the task you need to complete.
- Set the timer (typical time is twenty-five minutes).
- Work on the task.
- Stop work when the timer dings and take a small break (around five to ten minutes).
- Move on to the next task on your list (or continue working on the same task), again with the timer set at twenty-five minutes.
- Continue this process until you complete four *pomodoros* (four twenty-five-minute segments), and then take a longer break.

There are some people who disagree with this method, saying that the required stop at the timer can break flow. Some say that the drawback of the Pomodoro method is also what makes it so effective; it helps manage distractions, but the periodic interruptions of deep work for short breaks can have an impact on flow and productivity.

My response? There's no solution that's 100%. You'll have to decide the right amount of time for your focused work and determine whether the frequent breaks energize you or impact your flow in a negative way.

Here are ways this method can be an extremely useful tool for you.

- **Specific task.** When you have a specific task you need to complete (let's say a proposal is due to a client), give yourself a specific amount of time to complete it. You will limit all other distractions, focus, and get it done.
- **Emails**. This is a great method for work emails. Give yourself a set amount of time (consider twenty-five minutes two to three times a day as needed) to plow through everything. For things that require a response that you can get to in that timeframe, give a detailed response. For those that would require more thought, consider sending a response that the email has been received and you will get back to them with a more detailed response shortly. When it doesn't require anything from you other than your attention or to file it, you may find that you can not only get through this task more quickly, but it doesn't make you lose your focus on deep work slots, getting rid of the temptation of checking emails.
- **Personal tasks.** Let's face it. There are times during business hours that we have to get some personal tasks done, such as setting up appointments for doctors, dentists, emailing teachers, or booking that massage. Give yourself "x" number of minutes and knock it all out at once. It's off your mind, off your plate, and planned. Quickly.

- **Deep work.** There are times when you will get into a flow and find that you don't need to break at twenty-five minutes and want to continue. Reset it if needed, but know that you're committing to at least that amount of time to keep your focus. I love what my book coach Cathy does. She will ask an author in a writing session, "How much time do you think you need for this section?" They will tell her, and then she will say "Go!" At the end of that time, if they need more time, she will repeat, "How much time do you need to finish it?" and then start the timer again. It helps them get through sections they're struggling with, and this approach can help with your deep work time as well.

- **Social media.** How much time do you spend on social media? Do you find yourself reaching instinctively for your phone to fill the time, without being cognizant of how many reels you sit through? Or, do you log on to LinkedIn during the day and engage with posts from people in your network? Be in charge of the time you spend on social media. Try setting a timer for a set amount of time to allow yourself either some healthy escapism, or to connect with other professionals throughout the day in your industry online. You can be present on a platform that could be important for you professionally without allowing it to be a time suck.

- **Learning how long tasks *actually* take.** When you implement time boxing, you will become uber aware of how long tasks actually take when you're focused. You will be able to estimate how long each task will take before you start, time yourself, and then, after doing this for a number of times, you'll know exactly how long it takes you to complete specific tasks so you'll know how much you can get accomplished with focused attention. Get in the practice of timing yourself. You can use a timer on your mobile device, go old school like the kitchen timer, or, better yet, invest around $10 a month in a time tracking tool like TMetric, Toggl, Harvest, or others that allow you to capture this information, store it, and refer to it to help accurately plan your time moving forward.

Stop and Reflect

1. Look at your to-do list. Write out the estimated time you'll need for each of the things listed.
2. Choose any one of those tasks. Set your timer for the time you estimated (or use the Pomodoro method and set it for twenty-five minutes).
3. See how long it actually took.
4. Move on to the next one.
5. Look at your plans for other days this week. Do you have time allotted for these tasks on those days as well? If so, did you allot the right amount of time per this timing experiment?

Task Batching

Task batching is the process of grouping similar tasks together to be completed consecutively. The idea behind this is that by reducing the need for mental context-switching, you optimize workflow, preserve mental energy, and cultivate a clearer focus on related tasks.

Group similar (smaller) tasks together and schedule a specific time block to complete them all at once. Take the time boxing example above about emails. Emails and social media together can be scheduled as a twenty-five minute block of time. Emails alone can take that time. A good friend of mine who owns a copywriting company has taken this even further by batching tasks into days that she calls "Theme Days:" "Client Monday," "Marketing Tuesday," "Delivery Wednesday," "Content Thursday," "Freedom Friday," and "Sanity Saturday/Sunday." It keeps her from having back-to-back meetings every day during the week and plans out the time she needs to work on important tasks for her business.

Also consider Jane's approach, who started blocking her time so she had uninterrupted work time in the morning for deep work. She was then also able to task batch internal meetings (with her direct reports, her colleagues, her manager) so they occurred in the afternoons. I actually do the same and chunk my meetings into certain days and certain times of the day; that has helped me tremendously. We'll discuss more in Chapter Twelve, "Communicating Your Priorities," about how to have these conversations with your managers and your team. For Jane—and me!— task batching and boxing time allows us to get more accomplished in our days. We are in one "mode" for a set amount of time, and then can shift to another, being more focused on each.

Stop and Reflect

1. Write out a list of your tasks and batch together those that are similar.
2. Think about how you currently structure your days. Are there opportunities to batch meetings with clients? Internal meetings with your team, boss, direct reports?
3. Is there an opportunity to block out specific days so that you don't have meetings every day of the week, allowing you to focus on priority projects and deep work?
4. Can you meet team/client expectations checking emails two to three times per day (and not having it open to ping you while you're focused on other areas)?
5. Make changes to your calendar to structure your day in a way that will help you be the most productive.

Stop Multitasking

Do you think you are one of those people who can keep a lot of balls in the air? I do. But, I have learned that I can't effectively do more than one thing at a time, at least, not as efficiently as I could if I'd focus. Spoiler alert. Neither can you.

Gloria Mark is a Chancellor's Professor at the University of California, Irvine's Donald Bren School of Information and Computer Science, and she's a leading expert on work. She's also the author of *Attention Span,* which reveals results from her decades of research into how technology affects our attention. The research she conducted shows that the average amount of time people spend on a single event before being interrupted and before switching to something else was **three minutes and five seconds.** What's more concerning, the interrupted work resumed, on average, in **twenty-three minutes and fifteen seconds.**

When we multitask, when we get interrupted (either by our own interruptions or others), it takes over *twenty-three minutes* to get back to where we were before the interruption. On top of that, you don't immediately go back exactly to what you were doing before the task. Typically, interruptions change your physical environment. For example, someone comes into your office and gives you a stack of papers, and, now that they're on your desk, the environment has changed and it's harder to get back mentally to where you were prior to the interruption.

> When we multitask, when we get interrupted (either by our own interruptions or others), it takes over *twenty-three minutes* to get back to where we were before the interruption.

Muli-tasking doesn't work. Take note of when you can feel yourself trying to do more than one thing at a time. Notice it. Change the behavior. Write down what else you need to do, plan time for it, and then allow your-self the amount of time you set for one task at a time. Then move to the next. Then the next. And so on.

Stop and Reflect

1. How can you communicate with your team that you're focused on something and unavailable for "x" amount of time? If you work in an office, even if you have a door, you likely know the couple of knocks preceding the inevitable, "Do you have a minute?" If you're in a cube or in an office, can you hang something outside that they know means you're working on something and you'll be avail-able when it's completed? Cathy hangs a door hanger on her door knob that says "Go Away! I'm Writing!" so her partner knows when she doesn't want to be interrupted. What can effectively get your point across?

2. If you communicate through a particular soft-ware/app/messaging tool/etc., can you create an auto-notification or status stating that your head is down on something and will reply when you are finished?

3. If you work in a place with a shared calendar, can you block the time with "Working on (xyz)" so peo-ple know you're occupied?

Do Not Do List

Even with the time management principles you implement in your day, there are times you may still feel like not one more friggin' thing can fit on your to-do list. We're wired to add more and more and more. Personally, professionally. It can be satisfying, but it can also be a *lot.*

Do you experience the dopamine hit when you check things off your to-do list? Isaiah said that he will sometimes even write down what he's already done to just feel the satisfaction of checking it off. I am guilty too, occasionally! But what we know is he—and you—don't need *more* on the list. Sometimes, you need to work on taking things off of it. If you're trying to have any type of balance and harmony, if you want to create time for personal and professional commitments and goals, you may want to consider a "do-**not**-do list."

Here are some things to consider putting on that list:

- **Ignoring prioritization.** Don't skip the process of prioritizing tasks. Focus on high-impact and high priority tasks.
- **Mindlessly planning/attending meetings.** Not all meetings are important. Not all require your attendance. We've gotten into a pattern of setting up a meeting and inviting people willy-nilly. Stop it. Ask ahead of time for an agenda. Ask what your role will be. Ask about the purpose. If it's not something you need to attend, don't, but do so respectfully and confirm with your team or managers. Constant meetings disrupt workflow.

- **Procrastinating.** Refrain from putting off important tasks—it's so easy to do when these smaller tasks can quickly be checked off! Set deadlines for yourself, and respect those as you would any other deadline.
- **Checking email constantly.** Already wrote about this above, but do not forget this item on your "do-not-do list." Instead, set aside a set number of times per day you'll check them and allow yourself to do deeper work when you're not always connected.
- **Saying "yes" to everything.** Don't overcommit by accepting every request or project that comes your way. Be selective and learn to say "no" when necessary.
- **Not giving in to unlimited browsing of social media.** Set aside time that you'll allow yourself to be on social media. It's hard to get out of the vortex when you're not intentional about how long you want to be there.
- **Not turning down offers of help.** When you really could use some help and you get an offer, start accepting it. Move from "no thanks," to "Thank you! Here's what I could use help with."

Have you heard of the "one in, one out" rule for physical items coming into a home? Try to focus on being more intentional about what needs to go on your list, and, for that reason, what needs to come *off of it* in order for that to happen.

Stop and Reflect

1. Look at your to-do list today.
2. Are both professional and personal priorities reflected on your list?
3. What can you take off of it today? What's not a priority?
4. If it doesn't need to be done today, does it need to be done? And if so, does it need to be done by *you*?
5. Is there anything on this list you can delegate?
6. What from the above can you put on your "do-not-do list?"
7. What else will you add?

Delegating

I'll just come right out and say this: I know delegation is hard for a lot of people. Been there. I understand. Truly.

I *also* know that, when you start delegating, you get *a lot* of time back. When you delegate, you get to put your energy into the things that you can uniquely accomplish for your company, your team, or your family. You get to focus on high-priority tasks that align with your experience. Your team gets to work on tasks that suit their skills and experience, and you—if you're in a leadership role—get to show them the level of trust that you put into their work.

I know some of you reading this book will be the person who delegates responsibilities, and I know others of you will be the person who gets the tasks. Regardless of which direction the delegation is going, it's important. The process of delegation allows the team to be more efficient, allows people to work on tasks that suit their skills and expertise level, and increases productivity. Effective delegation builds teams. So, what are the reasons some are reluctant to delegate? Here's what I've both heard and said (many times):

"It's hard to explain, so I'll just do it myself."

"It'll just be faster if I just do it myself."

"I don't even have time to start thinking about what I *could* delegate."

"Training takes too long to get someone up and running to do all the things I *could* take off my plate."

"It's just uncomfortable asking someone else to take things off my plate."

That last one especially resonates with me. I felt like I was acting like a queen asking my loyal subjects to do my bidding. I was *so* uncomfortable at first asking people to take certain tasks off of my plate, until I did the exercise below and realized I was spending *way* more time than I should have in areas that would never grow the business. I put a hard line around what I should be doing (most of the time; we all roll up sleeves when needed), and asked my team to hold me accountable. I told them the reason I wouldn't be doing tasks I previously did is that there were others on the team who were faster, more efficient, quite frankly *better* in some areas, and, by spending my time there, I was doing a disservice to our company and stalling our growth.

When you honestly state why you're not going to do tasks you used to do and the benefits of you not doing them, I've found that teams will understand and support you.

I own a market research company. It doesn't make sense for me to learn how to scrub a list of email addresses for a large survey send. People on my team can do that a lot faster. It doesn't make sense for me to go back and forth on my availability for a client meeting. It makes more sense for my administrative assistant to do that, so I can focus on what I'll *present* at the meeting. Same goes for booking travel, ordering supplies, etc. I have an excellent administrative assistant with loads more experience in these areas than I do, and when I add up her hours each week, the reality is, if she wasn't doing this work, I would be doing it, and I wouldn't be able to spend time on the initiatives that will grow my business.

So, my advice: If you're delegating new tasks, start with an explanation of why you are doing this, what that time will allow you to focus on, why you're asking that person, what they'll be able to demonstrate by doing that task well, and then be very clear on what—exactly—the task is. In my experience , starting with *why* is always the way to go.

Stop and Reflect

1. Identify tasks suitable for delegation. Make a list of everything that you can think of that's currently on your plate that someone else on your team could (with training) take over. What's taking you time but not moving your initiatives forward?

- Consider complex projects you're working on where specific components could be delegated to team members who excel in these areas. It's a comprehensive approach *and* capitalizes on team members' individual strengths. Winning combo.

2. Write out any specialized tasks that you currently manage that require unique skills or expertise. Consider delegating to a team member who has these same skill sets.

3. Where do you currently feel overwhelmed? During peak periods where deadlines are looming, tasks can be distributed among team members to prevent burnout and maintain a balanced workload. Our team, in every morning huddle, answers whether they are at, under, or over capacity. Those who are under capacity can step in to support those feeling overwhelmed.

4. Choose team members with the skills and capacity for those tasks. You may think about who already has experience and could easily take these tasks over. You may also think about who this may be a stretch for, providing a growth or professional learning opportunity for someone on your team.

5. Clearly communicate expectations, deadlines, and any specific instructions. If there's a way you want it done, or you want it done by a certain time, be very clear.

6. **Start**. If you've just done the work and created the tasks, thought about the team members who could take them on, and know what the expectations will be, don't procrastinate any more on

delegating. You can get a lot of time back to focus on your high priority items when these tasks are off your plate.

Daily and Weekly Reflection

You started this chapter reflecting on what you haven't been able to find time for, and then I shared a number of strategies you can employ to effectively plan and block your time, batch your tasks, all for one reason: to give you the ability to make time for what's most important to you.

> Soon you will create time that you didn't realize was available to help you hit your personal and professional goals.

A critical component is taking time at the end of each day to reflect on where your time was spent and how you feel about that time allocation. Were you able to accomplish your top priorities? If yes, what was effective? If no, why not? What got in your way? What changes might you have to implement the following day? How do you feel about where you spent your time? Ask yourself the same types of questions at the end of each week as you prepare for the next, and, soon, I'm confident you'll create time that you didn't realize was available to help you hit your personal and professional goals.

In this chapter, we dove into ways to create time in your day to meet your goals. In the next chapter, we'll discuss what you may need to *stop* doing in order to make sure you can meet them. We'll discuss *hard stops*.

Chapter 11

Implementing Hard Stops and Removing Obstacles

"You can't reach for anything new if your hands are still full of yesterday's junk."

– Louise Smith

You've done a lot of work in this book to get here. You've assessed where you are now, set goals for where you want to be, and you've found time in your life to get there. You can create time to live intentionally. You can work towards these goals.

We opened the book with Jane, who was struggling. She started implementing the steps discussed throughout this book to help her focus on her priorities, set her goals, and find time in her day to do what's meaningful for her.

Even armed with this information, and, now, with the tools for continued self-reflection, what might get in her way to take her off this path?

Most importantly, what might get in *your* way?

There may be things that you do now, habits that you have that have formed over many years, relationships that you have that, quite honestly, aren't suiting you. They may be holding you back from where you want to go.

The reality is that you can't keep piling on more and more of what you want to do without taking some of the things that get in your way off of your plate. You may have to take stock of what in your life isn't suiting you and put *hard stops* in place where needed.

In this chapter, I'll share some common *hard stops* to help you get started. This list is by no means compre-hensive. Many of them may also not resonate with you. That's okay. The idea is to start identifying (or creating) your own *hard stops* that you need to put in place to get from where you are to where you want to go. There are more resources that are available online to help you work through this.

Mindless Scrolling

We are constantly connected. According to a Pew Research study from 2021, three in ten U.S. adults say they are "almost constantly online." In 2022, the global average daily social media usage of internet users worldwide amounted to 151 minutes per day. That's two hours and thirty-one minutes of watching other people's lives on the internet.

It's no surprise that research further shows that peo-ple who spend more time on their devices scrolling their phones for extended periods of time face an elevated risk of experiencing depression, anxiety, and loneliness.

Think about this. How many times a day do you reach for your phone out of habit? How frequently do you sit in your car, waiting to pick someone up, and start to scroll through TikTok, or Facebook, or Instagram?

Do you grab your phone and get on social media before you're out of bed?

Do you find yourself grabbing it even in the middle of the night when you get up to quickly go to the bathroom?

Do you fall asleep after scrolling through your phone at night?

How many times do you scroll without any awareness of the time you've been sucked into reels/tweets/updates/TikToks/etc.?

If your social media usage is average, there's over **two and a half hours a day** that is available to you, should you decide to take it, to start using more intentionally.

We lament that "there's no time." Mindless scrolling is a time suck. Here are ways to get hours back into your life every day.

- **Become intentional about your usage.** Decide when, where, and in what ways you want to engage with social media. If you want to scroll mindlessly through TikTok as an escape during your day, that's your choice. No judgment. But decide for yourself if that's your intention, or if you want to use that time differently. Become conscious of the usage and make the best decision for yourself and where you want to go.

- **Set daily limits.** How long will you allow yourself to be on social media per day? This is your *choice*. Monitor what you're doing now and create a goal for your usage.
- **Turn off notifications.** Nothing sucks you in like notifications. They prioritize other people over your time. If you set your intentions and have your time limit, you don't need notifications. You'll get on when you want to.
- **Nightly wind down.** The National Sleep Foundation recommends that you should stop using electronic devices for at least thirty minutes before bedtime. Instead, grab a book you've been wanting to read and start reading before bed.
- **Delete social media apps.** You may find it's a lot easier to not get sucked into social media when you don't have the buttons easily available. If you're having a hard time not relying on social media to fill your time, this is a way to get back some control.
- **Determine the purpose of your apps.** A good friend is credited with this bullet, which I would have overlooked. Be intentional about the purpose of an app for you. For example, my friend mentioned that, on Facebook, "I'm connected to every person I ever went to first grade with, shared a summer job with, etc., and I *never* go on that app because there's simply too much clutter—but I don't want to let go of the connections."

Alternatively, she uses Instagram much more intentionally and only follows people who are in her life currently, who she respects, finds inspirational, and wants to see in her feed more regularly. You "get out what you put in," as the saying goes, and that's no different with social media apps. Know their purpose for you.

- **Replace social media apps with helpful apps.** Best part: you decide what's a helpful app for you. Want to journal more? Learn another language? Listen to interesting audio books or podcasts? Delete and replace with what's important to you.
- **Take time out.** Pick a day and completely unplug. See how you fill your time. Maybe it's active. Maybe your brain just needs a break from everything and you're staring out the window, drinking a coffee and slowing down. Whatever it is, just unplug for a bit. Check in with yourself about what you miss about being online. Check in about what you gain from having the time offline. Noticing the positives makes it easier to want to continue the practice.

🛑 Limiting Yourself

"I could never do that."
"I'm not good at _____."
"I wouldn't even know where to start."
"I've never _____."

We tell ourselves a lot of self-narratives—about who we are, about what we're capable of, about what we're good at (and in turn, what we're not good at), about "the way we've always been," and "the way we've always done things."

Many times, that voice—and that self-awareness—is a positive thing. It can help us be more cognizant of our unique skills, personality attributes, and strengths. It can help us be more aware of what makes us who we are.

But our inner voice can also be a pretty big "B" sometimes.

I know mine can.

We compare ourselves to others and remind ourselves of what we can't do.

We remind ourselves of the way we've always done things, and tell ourselves that's the only way we know.

As I'm writing this book, building my business, and focusing on my family, my inner voice will tell me that I'm "getting too big from my britches." This voice is annoying, but it's there. It's something I have to work through.

Our inner voice can work to limit us, to maintain our status quo, to keep things as they are.

That is, unless we're aware of it, recognize it for what it is, and give ourselves a *different* narrative.

Katie's voice was a constant for years, making her question whether she could really do what she wanted to do. Become a single mother? Have a second child? Leave the comfort of a stable job to start her own business?

A voice was there. "You can't. This is too hard. It's too much."

Until she decided that she could, it wasn't, and she'd make it happen.

I loved the story she shared in the moment a massive dream of hers was coming true. She was in labor with her first child and cried out to her doula, "I don't think I can do this!"

Her doula replied, "You're already doing it."

And so can you.

Stop and Reflect

1. What do you see others doing that maybe you'd be interested in, but say, "Nah, that's not for me?" Write out some examples. Want to take a cooking class, but that's not "you?" Want to learn how to sew, but you "should have done this years ago, and it's too late?" Want to start being more physically active and run a 10k? Sky's the limit.

2. Recognize where you're putting blockers on yourself. Are you telling yourself you can't do these things before you start because they don't fit the narrative of who you think you are or what you think you are capable of?

🛑 Carrying the Weight of Other People's (Perceived) Opinions

Giving a *%& about what other people think is exhausting. Giving a *%& about what other people think when you've decided to make changes to your life and become more intentional about who you are and where you want to go can be oppressive.

Not everyone is going to support you, for a whole host of reasons. Most of these reasons have more to do with them than with the person making the change. Not everyone is doing the same type of work that you are. Not everyone is on a personal or professional development journey, or wants to get more intentional about the life they're creating. Other people may not understand your desire for this path. They may not support it out of fear. They may not want you to change or to grow because it may change the relationship they have with you. They may feel more distanced from you as you grow. They may be intimidated by this type of self-development because, for their own reasons, they're not ready to go there themselves.

And this isn't your problem.

Worrying about what other people will think about your decisions will not help you make better decisions for *your* life.

Worrying about what other people will think about your decisions can stifle the direction that *you* are meant to go.

Their reaction to your self-development journey says more about them than it does about you.

We all have phases of our lives, and there are people who will put us in a box from the time they knew us "when." I've felt this. I've gone from being the life of the party in my twenties to focusing more on my career and my personal relationships in my thirties (while still having fun, thank you very much!), to, in my forties, figuring out how to balance a big career while making time for my marriage and the little people that I brought into the world.

> Their reaction to your self-development journey says more about them than it does about you.

There are people that I know from my twenties who probably like that version of me a *whole* lot better than they'd like me now. There are those people who knew me who can't relate to the person who now gets up at 5:30 AM to write or exercise to get my day started, because it likely doesn't sound nearly as fun as closing down a local bar and grabbing greasy food at a drive-through before sleeping in the next day until noon. But that's who I have become. That's what I enjoy doing *now,* and I have to shed the feelings of discomfort that there are people who knew me who liked me more *then*. Who don't get who I am now. Who likely, if I'm honest, I don't have much in common with anymore.

I have had to ignore the snide comments from people who say, "Who does she think she is?" and just let comments roll off my back while I focus on building my business, writing this book, and living my life the way I want.

I'm not saying it's easy. It's a hard realization, at times, that some people in your life will be there forever, and some will only be there for certain phases, and they'll have a snapshot of those phases and keep you in that place.

Think about what—and who—serves you where you are *now*, and where you want to go.

Be aware of the weight of other people's opinions and what they mean to you. Also recognize that this may just be your inner voice, filling in a narrative you *think* they're saying. I've had full on conversations with people in my head who never once attacked me or criticized my decisions, but I was prepared to give "my side of the story." Just be aware of this. Only then can you work to overcome it.

> Think about what—and who—serves you where you are *now*, and where you want to go.

Stop and Reflect

1. Write or take time to think about the different phases of your life and who you were at those times.
2. In your life, who still associates you with these times and won't accept where you're seeking to go?
3. Who will accept the changes you're making?
4. Take the time to recognize the support you have (and don't have) from those currently in your life.

Apologizing for What You Want

You do not have to apologize for wanting more in life.

This bears repeating. You do not have to apologize, to *anyone*, for wanting more out of your life.

This story has always resonated with me on this topic.

Christina's family had always expected her to become a lawyer. Her parents were both lawyers, as was her grandfather—he started the firm where her family worked. She spent her summers in high school going into the office to get experience, and she started college in the pre-law track because she knew it is what everyone wanted from her.

But she knew it wasn't what she wanted to do. Her heart wasn't in it. Her passion was tinkering out in their garage, always making things, taking things apart, and putting them back together. She loved her engineering and math courses in high school and was drawn to the idea of being a software engineer.

To say her decision to not follow the lawyer path was met with resistance would be a massive understatement.

She could have a job immediately upon passing the bar. How many people have that opportunity? She would be able to continue in the family business and pass it on to her children in the future. How could she selfishly walk away from this amazing opportunity they're providing her? She would change her mind later. She would see that software engineering isn't all it's cracked up to be, and she would come back to them, admitting she was wrong.

It wasn't pretty.

There was nothing wrong with her family wanting her to follow in their footsteps and join a lucrative career. But there was also nothing wrong with her deciding it wasn't the life *she* wanted to live.

It took her a long time to realize she shouldn't have to apologize for wanting more or for wanting to do something different with her life.

She shouldn't have to explain why the path they laid out for her didn't suit her. She shouldn't have to justify why it wouldn't help her become the person she wanted to become.

> Stop apologizing for putting yourself first. You deserve to.

Not everyone got it. Not everyone supported her decision. And she knew people felt she was being selfish in the decision she made.

Be selfish. Be good to people. Be honest, be transparent, be empathetic, but stop apologizing for wanting to live your life on your terms. Stop apologizing for putting yourself first. You deserve to.

Stop and Reflect

1. Write or take time to think about this section.
2. What resonates with you?
3. Do you feel you have to justify why you want changes in your life?
4. Who are the voices that are keeping you down the most?
5. What do you think they would say to you?
6. What would you want to say to them?

Feeling Guilty for Saying "No"

If you want to live *your* best life, you have to start embracing how to say "no" without feeling guilty.

I know. Just reading that probably feels uncomfortable.

How many times have you said "yes" to projects that you didn't have time for? Gone out for an evening when you really wanted to sit at home and read a book or catch up on laundry? Donated to a charity you didn't even feel that strongly about because you didn't want to look someone in the eye and say "no thanks?"

Guilty. I'm as guilty as everyone, and it's a constant work in progress to say "no" without guilt.

We are socialized to be helpful and to not want to disappoint other people. But if you put everyone else's needs first, take a moment to think about where that means you're putting your own needs.

Second? Last?

That's what needs to change.

Here are some ways to stop feeling you need to say "yes" when you want to say "no"—and feel better doing it.

- **Know your intentions and priorities.** When you know yourself—your limitations, your priorities, your other commitments, what you like and dislike, how you have already decided you want to spend your previous time—all of that is *key* to being able to discern what types of requests are worth entertaining or considering, and which don't align with *you* and what you are able or willing to offer. Every other strategy I'll provide below for how to say "no" stems from this. The work you did up to this point should make you feel confident in stating what you *do* and *don't* want to do. Want to go to a fundraiser on Saturday night for a charity you've never heard of with a lot of people you don't know? "No, thank you. I have a big hike planned with the kids and need to get up early Sunday to write." My priorities include lots of time with my kids and writing this book. I can much more easily say "no" to something that takes me away from what I want to focus on. I put in the work (as did you!) to know these priorities, so, no apologies for protecting my time.

- **Keep it short.** You don't have to come up with 1,000 excuses as to why you don't want to do something. "Want to go to the beach this weekend?" "No, thanks." "Want to go to a movie next week?" "I appreciate you asking, but no thank you." I know it can feel uncomfortable just reading this but, believe it or not, no further explanation is required on your part if you don't want to do something! "No thank you" is a full sentence. Embrace that, as uncomfortable as it may feel.

- **Be as direct as you want to be.** None of Jaime's friends will ever ask her to watch their cat when they're away because—she'll admit it—she's super awkward with cats and doesn't want to be around them. She loves dogs, but was bitten as a kid and is still a bit squeamish about trying to be the alpha, so she recognizes she shouldn't be a dog walker or responsible for taking care of her friend's fur babies. She just isn't comfortable. She doesn't want to. Her schedule on the weekends is usually pretty intense, and she doesn't want to factor someone's furry family member into the equation. That may sound harsh, but it isn't. She knows this about herself and now can comfortably say when people ask her to pet sit, "Sorry I can't help, but this just isn't for me. I think someone else would be much better suited for this." Those who know her well now know not even to ask. She was direct the first time, and it stuck.

- **Pause.** Saying "no" outright can feel extremely uncomfortable. Know that you don't have to say "no" outright, you can give yourself some time to consider. "Let me check with my calendar at home to see what we have going on that day" or "Let me check in with (partner) to see if we have anything happening that day" are ways to bide time to think about an answer, but don't take away your own agency or put the responsibility on someone else. This works well in professional settings as well. Someone wants you to take on a new project or responsibility? "Let me take some time to think about this and I'll get back to you. I just want to make sure that I can meet the responsibilities that I already have on my plate before committing" is a lot better than saying "yes" and not being able to deliver, or automatically saying "no" without giving something the consideration it may require.

- **Consider the context.** I just used the dog-sitting example above, but, honestly, if a close friend with a dog had an emergency and needed her help, Jaime would jump in immediately to help. I'm sure you would, too, in similar circumstances. That's why circumstances and context matter. Consider the relationship, the importance of the relationship, the urgency of the request, and your unique ability to be able to support before answering.

- **Be prepared for the reaction of others (or be prepared to accept "no," too).** I acknowledge it is hard to say "no," and I'm guessing you likely felt the sting of just hearing "no thanks" without a bunch of excuses intertwined. Know that "no" isn't always comfortable for the person hearing it, either. So, if you're making steps to start getting more comfortable saying "no," you have to be comfortable hearing it, too, and accepting when others show their limits.
- **Acknowledge your emotions,** but own what you want to do.
- **Journal it.** Work through it. It's uncomfortable. Writing it out helps.
- **Be firm.** It's *your* time. It's *your* decision. Hold to what *you* want to do.

Comparing Yourself to Others

In a world of constant scrolling, unlimited photoshopped and touched-up images on Instagram, and regular posts from their network on LinkedIn who are clearly *killing it* in their professional careers, it's no surprise people may feel like massive failures for not having started and sold their own companies for millions of dollars before they hit the ripe age of thirty and make it onto a "thirty under thirty" list full of the *amazing* things they're doing. Blargh.

It's natural to compare yourself to others. There's even a psychological term for it: *social comparison theory*, which was coined in the 1950s by psychologist Leon Festinger. The idea is that people determine their own worth based on how they stack up against others.

It can be beneficial. When we compare ourselves to others as a way of measuring our personal development or for motivation to change areas of our lives, this type of comparison can have a positive impact. When I first read about Sarah Blakely, the founder of Spanx, starting out in a one-room apartment and getting told "no" over and over, and then building a billion dollar brand, her story was an inspiration for me.

But if you're not mindful that you're making comparisons, there can be a negative impact as well. You can see how well it appears others are doing and feel like you're not successful enough, not thin enough, not rich enough, not social enough, not educated enough, not experienced enough, not (fill in the blank). Maybe you seek out comparisons. When you want to feel better about yourself, you compare yourself to people who are doing worse off than you are in certain areas. It's something we do! While we don't seek to make ourselves feel bad, studies have found that, while people who regularly compare themselves to others may find some motivation in personal development and improvement, they are also more likely to experience feelings of deep dissatisfaction, guilt, and remorse.

When you're on this road to self-discovery, to living more intentionally, your only litmus test is how **you** are progressing every day and how that progression makes **you** feel.

Stop and Reflect

Do you think that you compare yourself to other people on a regular basis? Take some time to jot out the positive and negative thoughts that you have based on these comparisons.

1. Are there particular people that you compare yourself to that act as an inspiration for you (Sarah Blakely example above)?
2. Are there people who you compare yourself to that make you feel more negatively about some aspect of yourself?
3. Write about what specifically makes you feel negatively in those comparisons.
4. What steps can you take (and *will* you take) to change this behavior?

Trying to Do It All (Something Has to Give)

You cannot do it all.

Rationally, you know this.

"Of *course* I can't do it all, Gina. Why even write that sentence?"

For one, as I shared earlier in the book, previous generations naturally had more defined boundaries between work and personal life. My parents went to work, then they went home. They weren't responding to messages on their devices while sitting in bed at the end of the night or reaching for their phones first thing in the morning. The expectation to be able to do it all is, in my humble opinion, somewhat generational. Gen X (hi!) was told that we could achieve an education, a successful career, a fulfilling marriage and family life, a beautiful home—do it *all*. This isn't just a Gen X'er problem. There are unreasonable expectations across later generations as well, with all of us feeling that we are being sent the message that we should be able to "do it all" professionally and personally.

Because, if you're like many of us, we blame ourselves when we can't do everything we think we should be. We've been sold a bill of goods with messages that we have received since, well, birth? We judge ourselves for our perceived inability to live up to what it seems like others are capable of doing when it looks like they all have their... ahem... *acts*... together and it *seems* like we don't.

A good friend said to me that intentionality feels so uncomfortable (and yet is so necessary) because it forces you to discern and articulate what is important to *you*. How you spend your hours, days, etc, in accordance with what's true and important to *you*. That's the purpose of this section. Recognizing that and realizing that something has to give.

> At these times, it's important to remember that what you do and how you spend your time is an intentional choice.

At these times, it's important to remember that what you do and how you spend your time is an intentional choice.

So is where you decide to *not* spend your time.

Maybe you are the person who loves to show off your creativity and love for your kids by creating amazingly creative, cute cut-out sandwiches that you can envision them opening up at their school lunch in front of their friends and smiling.

Maybe you're the person who throws a sandwich, an apple, some pretzels or chips, and a piece of fruit into a brown paper bag and calls it a day.

Who is being the better parent to their kid?

Maybe you're the person who will painstakingly plan out every detail of a party that you're going to throw, ensuring that you have the menu just so, planning out the music you'll play, and planning the seating arrangements.

Maybe you're the person who invites people over for a potluck and BYOB and puts up lawn chairs in the back-yard for a casual get-together.

Who throws the better party?

Obviously, there's no right answer. Even if you lean one way or another, there are different ways that you can approach just about anything.

And everything that you do is a choice, made using your time, your energy, and demonstrates what you care most about.

You make choices every day about where you'll spend your time. You also make choices about where you will *not*.

You look at your priorities and you determine what will get your time.

If spending hours planning out an elaborate dinner party is worth your time, you'll do it. If you decide that you want to spend that time another way, you may opt for a more low-key get-together.

Choices.

You cannot do everything. There are trade-offs. Your time and energy are finite. So, you choose.

You may do a little economy lesson of opportunity cost in your head. "What does participating in this one thing or this choice, require me to miss/forsake?" And, "How do I feel about that?"

I know that my parties will never be the talk of the town. My lunches for my kids will be subpar. I'm the one who throws a sandwich into a brown paper bag if they don't get lunch at school. My kids aren't envied by their friends at lunch for the cute presentation. I know this. I accept it. These are just two small examples, but multiply them by all the things we have on our plates. By choosing what we will do and what we will scale down, **we create time for ourselves.**

The time we spend in areas we don't care about impacts the time we have for our priorities.

Stop and Reflect

1. What brings you stress, and no joy?
2. Where can you say to yourself, "Something has to give, and this is it?"
3. Jot out some of the areas where you can choose to not care as much as you have previously.
4. Think about what that will allow you more time to focus on.
5. *Choose.*

Apologizing for Seeking Balance

I'm going to let you in on a few secrets.

You can be a committed employee *and* want to be present for your family for more than an hour a day.

You can deliver exceptional results *and* make time for what's important to you personally.

You can be promoted and move up in your career without sacrificing your mental, physical, and emotional health.

Gone are the days (or long gone *should* be the days) where we glorify over-working, where we pride ourselves on how busy we are and how much time we spend in the office. If that's what you want to do, great. You'll always hear me talking about choices. But, if that's not what you want, you're not less committed to your employer because you want to develop in other ways personally, or have time to spend on hobbies that you like outside of work.

What if we embraced that we can be committed employees *while* showing that we're full humans with interests outside of a nine-to-five? In Chapter Twelve, "Communicating Your Priorities," I'll share how to have those conversations, how to show you're committed while also wanting to focus on what matters to you personally.

Where I've seen this happen frequently is with new parents. According to The Mom Project, 43% of highly skilled women leave the workforce after becoming mothers. *Forty-three percent*! This resonates with me because I've been there. I've wondered how I could possibly manage the responsibilities of a managing director at a

Fortune 500 company while parenting in the way that I wanted to. I was told I could make it work. I was told there would be support. I know there were good intentions, but I just didn't feel I could make it work the way *I* needed it to. I left to create my own company so I could create that type of culture.

Professional success *and* work-life balance.

Hitting client deliverables *and* showing up for my kids' after school activities.

They're not mutually exclusive.

This is worth a pause, as "balance" means many things to many people, and there's no "right" answer for what balance *is*, nor what it *should be*. Work-life balance refers to equilibrium and the harmonious integration of professional and personal aspects of a person's life. It means that you should be able to effectively manage the demands of your career while also nurturing relationships, pursuing hobbies, and attending to your physical and mental well-being. The goal is to allocate time and energy to various facets of life to prevent one from dominating or overshadowing the others.

There's just no uniformity of what that right balance is or should be.

I've found that I don't achieve balance every day. Some days, I have to focus more on work for a tight deadline; sometimes I need to take off work to be the chaperone for my kid's field trip. Sometimes I need to shut it all down and go on a hike to clear my head.

Balance may not be possible to feel *every day*, but to me, being intentional, being *aware* of how I'm spending my time and how it's being allocated across all that's important to me, has helped me feel more centered, calm, and "balanced" on a more regular basis. I may be working twelve hours today, but I'm making that *choice*, because that's what's required today (or this week), but I'll work to balance things out next week so I don't burn out and neglect other priorities.

> You get to define what balance looks like for you.

You get to define what balance looks like for you.

You don't need to apologize or feel like you're less than—or not as committed, driven, focused—because you want to feel contentment professionally *and* personally.

Stop and Reflect

1. How do you define balance?
2. What makes you feel balanced?
3. How do you course correct if you start feeling unbalanced?
4. Do you feel like you're torn between being the employee/leader that you want to be and making time for your personal goals and priorities? If so, where's the pull?
5. What feels off-balance?

 Slacking on Sleep

Jane was fall-down tired every night. She would crash on the couch, put on Netflix to spend time with her husband watching their favorite show together, but then pass out, waking up only to wash her face, brush her teeth, and go to bed, where she would toss and turn until the morning, waking up tired.

What about you? Do you plan your sleep, or do you let it just happen when and where it comes?

Here's the thing. **You know sleep is important.** You know, rationally, that sleep is good for you, but why, then, isn't it more of a priority? Why does it get put on the back-burner of habits that you know promote health?

This was an area Jane decided to focus on when she started her intentionality practice. Prior to having kids, she and her husband would work late, eat late, arrive back home and sleep later than she is able to now. Their days started and ended later. Having kids just blew that right up. All of the sudden, there were people in the house who required her attention from the time they got up until the time they went to bed, and if she wanted to focus on sleep and get eight hours of sleep per night, that meant that she would have to fall asleep by 11:30 PM to be ready to get up with them by 7:30 AM.

She quickly realized, though, that she didn't want to wake up and immediately begin taking care of other people. She wanted to carve out some time for herself in the morning to start walking; she was lacking in the exercise department. She wanted to start the day with time for herself, reading, meditating, journaling. She wasn't concerned about what exactly she was doing for that time, she just didn't want to start off working and mom-ing from the moment she woke up.

She decided to give herself an hour every morning before the kids were up. They wake up at 7:30 AM, so she committed to doing something for *herself* every day at 6:30. To prioritize sleep, that meant she had to start her sleep routine by 10:00 PM, so she could be asleep by 10:30 to get eight hours.

She had it planned out. She was finally going to have this time for herself! She was finally going to start the day making herself a priority. She was finally going to prioritize getting some exercise and a good night's sleep.

Then her husband got upset.

All of the sudden, she wasn't available to stay up late with him. Their nightly routine of watching shows until they fell asleep no longer worked for her. He felt like she was no longer making him a priority. She was changing the habit they started *together*—watching their favorite shows when the kids fell asleep. Prioritizing sleep meant deprioritizing the time she was able to spend with her husband, and that was a tough change. For both of them.

She needed to find other times to spend with him during the week other than late at night, and he needed to understand that his wife having time alone benefited her, which also benefited him—and the whole family.

I always read about creating healthy sleep habits, but wanted to share this story about Jane and her husband because what I don't typically see in the conversation about sleep is any acknowledgement of the types of changes it may cause in your routine, and for others in your family. Acknowledge that first—and the discomfort it may bring, the conversations you may need to have—and then put some of these tips in place to help you build better sleep habits.

- **Maintain a consistent sleep schedule.** Try going to bed and waking up at the same time each day, even on the weekends. Consistency helps regulate your body's internal clock, making it easier to fall asleep and wake up naturally.
- **Create a relaxing bedtime routine.** Engage in calming activities before bed to signal to your body that it's time to wind down. Read a book, practice gentle yoga, or take a warm bath. Jane used to crash while watching TV. Now, she reads for a half hour after washing her face and brushing her teeth. The consistency is calming.
- **Optimize your sleep environment.** Make your sleep environment conducive to *rest*. Ensure your bedroom is dark, quiet, and at a comfortable temperature. Investing in a comfortable mattress and pillows can significantly improve your sleep quality.
- **Limit screen time before bed.** The blue light emitted by screens (phones, tables, computers, TVs) can interfere with your body's production of the sleep-inducing hormone melatonin. That's not even mentioning how easy it is to get sucked into reels and letting time pass. Aim to avoid screens at least an hour before bedtime.
- **Watch your diet and caffeine intake.** Avoid heavy meals, caffeine, and large amounts of liquid close to bedtime. These can disrupt your sleep by

causing discomfort, increasing the need to wake up to use the bathroom, or interfering with your ability to sleep.

- **Limit alcohol before sleep.** Alcohol impacts quality of sleep. It may sound counterproductive to those of us who have had a few drinks and fallen asleep soundly, completely foregoing the nightly routine. But you "pay for it" the second half of the night. Alcohol is initially sedating, but as it's metabolized, it's very activating. You may crash, then toss and turn the second half of the night, impacting your ability to get a good night's sleep.

Give yourself some grace as you focus on implementing best practices to foster a healthy sleep habit because, while all these are helpful, they may be hard at first to implement and stick with. As I write this chapter, I stayed up late last night watching a movie with my husband after having a couple of glasses of wine at dinner, royally failing on #1, #2, #4, #5, and #6. That's fine. That's life. I prioritized time together more than my standard time to sleep. You'll make those same types of adjustments. Acknowledge that, and start anyway. Then work on holding yourself accountable by how you're doing each week.

Stop and Reflect

1. What sleep habit will you commit to starting this week?
2. Write out your sleep routine. What time will you start going to bed? How much time do you require

per night to sleep? What will be your typical wake-up time?
3. Put a note on your calendar for next week to see how you are doing on your sleep habit commitment.

🛑 Not Focusing on Your Physical Health

When you don't feel well, it's hard to live your life as fully as possible. Until she implemented changes, Jane was going off little sleep, grabbing a muffin and caffeine on the way to work, getting takeout for lunch, grabbing more caffeine and a sweet for an afternoon pick-me-up, and focusing on getting her family to their activities rather than finding time in her day to move. In this one example, there are a number of National Health Institute recommendations that she hasn't followed.

Being mindful of what you put into your body, how physically active you are, and your weight is critical for making sure your body is working properly. These habits lower risk of disease, increase energy, lower stress, improve your brain health, help manage weight, strengthen bones and muscles, and improve your ability to not only do, but *enjoy*, more everyday activities.

You know it's important. So, why don't you focus more on your physical health?

Habits, for one. Maybe you weren't raised in a household where these habits were a priority. What's that adage? Old habits die hard. They do, but they can change. You are not a victim to the habits that

When you decide you want to make a change, you can.

you built throughout your life. **When you decide you want to make a change, you can.** That's where reading this book comes in. By acknowledging you want a change, you can start.

Our environment is a huge factor. When you're surrounded by other people who are making their physical health a priority, it's a lot easier to keep on track. That's why many weight loss programs recommend joining with a friend or having a community to help you keep going, as it's not easy to make such a big change.

If you're ready to focus on making positive changes to your physical well-being, you don't need a laundry list containing everything to consider. Start with these four steps when beginning your physical health journey:

- **Get active.** Moving more and sitting less can have major health benefits. The Center for Disease Control and Prevention states that adults need 150 minutes of moderate-intensity physical activity and two days of muscle strengthening activity per week. If that sounds like a lot, it breaks down to twenty minutes a day. And if that sounds daunting, that can be broken down into four five-minute bouts of movement per day. The activity doesn't all have to come at the same time. Find ways to take stretch breaks: park a little further when you run errands or take a five-minute walk around your block as a break.
- **Build and maintain your muscle.** Strength training may enhance your quality of life and improve your ability to do everyday activities. It protects your body from wear and tear, contributes to

better balance, and may reduce risks of falls as you age. If there's one area that people find the most intimidating, it's starting to lift weights when they don't have experience, or walking into a gym where they feel out of their element. At many of the gyms around the country, there are personal trainers there to help you get started and who are welcoming to new members taking positive steps to improve their health. Don't let intimidation get in your way of such an important aspect of your physical health.

- **Find a healthy weight.** Keeping your body at a healthy weight can help stave off type 2 diabetes, certain cancers that occur due to excess weight, high blood pressure, high cholesterol, heart disease, gallstones, osteoarthritis, breathing problems, sleep apnea—the list continues. There are tools to determine your ideal weight, like the Body Mass Indicator, but there is disagreement among medical experts about the usefulness of this and other tools, as no one tool can tell a person their exact health status. The steps outlined in this section will help move towards a healthy weight, but if you're unsure as to what that should be, it's best to discuss with your doctor.

- **Eat a healthy diet.** Eating a healthy diet offers a wide range of benefits with regard to your physical health, but also your mental and emotional well-being. A healthy diet will help you maintain a healthy weight or reach your desired weight goals, providing necessary nutrients while controlling calorie intake, reducing the risk of obesity and related health issues. It improves heart health, reduces risk of chronic disease, promotes better digestive health, a stronger immune system, enhanced cognitive function, improved mood and mental health, increased energy, a longer life span—and that's not even mentioning the positive impact on the environment.

Starting something new isn't easy. Starting a physical health goal is an important step towards better health and a more fulfilling life, but it also comes with its own set of challenges, ranging from lack of motivation to time constraints, physical limitations, perceived lack of skill/ability, exercise-related discomfort, lack of social support, self-consciousness, inconsistent progress, and so on.

There are challenges. Acknowledge them. Start anyway.

Consider starting with small, achievable goals, seeking guidance from fitness professionals or friends with experience, and finding activities you genuinely enjoy. If I had to run on a treadmill every day of my life, I'd tap out. That's not for me, and I have friends who have trained on a treadmill for a marathon watching their favorite shows. **Find what works for *you*.** Build a support network, track your progress, and be patient with yourself. Give yourself some grace. You're starting something new, something difficult, but the payoffs are huge.

> There are challenges. Acknowledge them. Start anyway.

Stop and Reflect

1. How will you start implementing changes in these four areas?
2. What's your goal this week to be more active?
3. How will you start building or maintaining muscle, if this is a part of your routine?
4. What is a healthy weight for you, and what steps can you implement to start making it a priority?
5. What changes do you want to implement in your day-to-day to eat a healthier diet?

Seeking Perfection

When writing this book my book coach said to me, "I want you to focus on sending me a shitty first draft," which she told me came from the book *Bird by Bird* by Anne Lamott, an excellent book about writing.

Admittedly, I didn't realize the power of the statement at the time, but I do now.

She knew I would do what I was doing—getting in my own way. She has worked with authors for years and knows what holds back their progress: **striving for perfection.**

I wanted every word to be right, so almost as soon as it was on paper, I was scrutinizing what I wrote. I was editing while writing, and not moving as quickly as I should have, until she freed me by saying, "Send me a shitty first draft."

Of course, I didn't intentionally want to give her a bad first draft, but it got me out of my way. When I couldn't find the exact word I wanted, or when I found I wasn't completely sure about how I wanted to tighten up a section or transition to the next topic, I just jotted in the margin, "come back to this when editing" and kept going.

It got me thinking, where might you be seeking perfection when starting something, and how might the perfection-seeking hold you back?

Have you felt you had to present yourself in a better place than you are out of fear for not being where you want to be and not wanting to lose face, or look like you have it all together?

Where might seeking perfection be holding you back?

Have you ever cleaned your house before your cleaners come?

Felt like you need to lose a few pounds to fit into some new workout clothes before you hit the gym?

Don't get me wrong. There are times that striving for perfection is not only a good thing, it's required. Professionally, we strive to do our best work and deliver our best work to our clients. If I have to have a surgery, I want that surgeon to be perfect. When I fly, I have the same expectations of the pilots. Striving for perfection is sometimes needed.

But striving for perfection when starting something new can hold you back. Do you have unrealistic expectations about what your first notes should sound like, how your first brush strokes should look on canvas when you start painting—Bob Ross made it look a lot easier than it is!—how you should feel starting a new exercise routine, and so on? When it's not perfect, instead of giving yourself the grace to recognize that starting new things can be hard and messy, but that you will get better, do you find yourself wanting to throw in the towel instead?

Acknowledge it. That's all. We do it. See where you can opt for 70% instead of perfection and see how that can free you, giving you the grace to try new things.

Stop and Reflect

1. Where is striving for perfection potentially holding you back?
2. What can be the equivalent of a "shitty first draft" in your life, regarding something new you want to start?
3. Where will you give yourself a little more grace to not be perfect, but simply trying to learn?

🛑 Not Focusing on Your Mental Health

Not to pick on Jane again (I do only because she represents so many of us, and she started us off on this book journey), but at the end of the day, she was fall-down tired, crashing in front of a TV in the evening on a regular basis after working all day and taking care of her family. She had been experiencing a constant lack of energy, seeing changes in her sleep patterns, slowly gaining weight, and was feeling something she had a hard time describing: easily agitated, frustrated. Small triggers were having an overexaggerated impact on her.

She wasn't taking care of her mental well-being.

She needed to make changes.

Focusing on our mental health is crucial. Just as you pay attention to what you put into your body and how physically active you are, taking care of your mental health is vital for a fulfilling life. Your mental well-being influences *every single aspect* of your life and your overall health.

> Your mental well-being influences *every single aspect* of your life and your overall health.

It's discussed more now than it ever has been, but some of us are reticent to talk about self-care, to be open about our mental health and what we need to maintain it.

Own it. Embrace it. You need to make time for yourself. You need to stop apologizing for self-care. You need to prioritize your mental well-being and commit to putting steps in place to ensure it *continues* to be a priority.

Here are some tips for focusing on your mental health journey.

- **Prioritize self-care:** You cannot get water from an empty well. Self-care is the practice of deliberately taking actions and making choices that promote and prioritize your physical, mental, and emotional well-being, so that you have water left to give. It's a proactive and intentional approach to maintaining and improving your overall health and quality of life. **Self-care is not a luxury;** it's a *fundamental* aspect of self-preservation and a key component of a balanced and healthy lifestyle. Self-care can take many forms, but, in short, it's time allocated for activities that help you relax, de-stress, and recharge. It's also highly

individualized, because what works for some people will naturally not work for others. Go online to
find a worksheet on various types of self-care and
suggestions on how to begin to implement them
regularly into your life.

- **Seek professional help.** If you're struggling with
mental health, **do not hesitate** to reach out to
a mental health professional. They can provide
guidance, therapy, or medication if needed.

- **Build a support network.** Sharing your feelings
and challenges with friends and family you trust is
therapeutic. Sometimes, just being able to vocalize what you're experiencing is what is needed.
That coffee with a friend or a drink after work may
seem like time you don't have in your schedule.
It's not a luxury. Support networks help us cope
with stresses in our lives.

- **Practice mindfulness.** We've focused a lot
already in this book on living more intentionally,
so we'll keep these tips short here, but know that
mindfulness and intentionality are key areas to be
focused on regarding your mental health.

- **Practice gratitude.** Cultivate a regular practice of
reflecting on what you're grateful for. This simple
practice that can be implemented into journaling,
meditating, or done as its own activity has a profound impact on shifting your focus from negative
thoughts to positive ones, improving your overall
mental well-being.

Most importantly: start. You're worth it. You deserve it.

Remember that your mental health journey is unique to you, and it may involve a combination of strategies and practices. It's essential to be patient with yourself, give yourself grace, seek professional help if needed, and continue to explore what works best for your mental well-being.

Most importantly: start. You're worth it. You deserve it.

🛑 Letting Alcohol and Drugs Get in Your Way

As I said in the opening of this book, I am not an expert in many areas; this includes substance and alcohol abuse or addiction. I do know that addiction is complicated and multi-faceted, so, while I wish this section could be a stronger resource for those who are experiencing alcohol and drug addiction, I acknowledge my lack of expertise in this area and recommend you seek out resources from professionals who specialize in those areas.

What I also know from experience, though, is that not all alcohol use is abuse. I will be the first to readily share that I like a glass of wine or two with friends, and enjoy a glass of wine while making dinner with my husband. I like a cold beer after a hike. I drink on occasion.

I've also found that this is an area where being more intentional and making deliberate choices that align with my values, goals, and priorities has made a profound impact.

For example, I found that my way of saying to a friend "I miss you. I'd love to get together," comes out instead "Hey—wanna to get a drink next week?" Likely a carry-over from many after-work happy hours, it's become an easy way to get together. An easy ask. An easy acceptance that leads to spending time together.

However, once I became aware of my tendency to immediately ask a friend for a drink when I really just wanted time together, I started asking friends if they wanted to meet for a walk or a hike. I still get that hour, hour plus with my friend. I still get the conversation that I'm craving and the connection, without relying on a beverage to get me there.

It's a seemingly small change, but big benefits.

I've also become intentional about being aware of how I feel after one drink, after two, three, more than three (spoiler: not great). I ask myself, "How do I want to feel tomorrow?" because a night out where I've had more than a couple of drinks will impact my next day. Is it worth it? Sometimes, maybe so. I may say a fun night with friends on occasion may be worth not waking up at 5:30 the next morning, ready to tackle the day. Sometimes, I'd like to get together, but have sparkling water. There isn't a right answer; the point is that my choice is *intentional.*

> When you overindulge one day, you are borrowing from the next.

When you overindulge one day, you are borrowing from the next.

Is it worth it for you?

It's a choice. It's *your* choice.

Have you ever paid attention to how you feel when you have one drink? Two? Three? Have you noticed how you *sleep* when you have one drink, two drinks? Have you noticed how you sleep when you have *none*? Have you paid attention to how motivated you feel the next day after you've had a few drinks?

The purpose of being intentional is being *aware* and then making the decisions that you want to make for your life.

I get to decide what I want my relationship with alcohol to be, and, unless there's addiction, you can, too.

I know that relationships with alcohol and drugs can be complicated. Self-reflection is an important step in recognizing what your relationship is. Asking yourself these questions can help you assess where you are and determine whether seeking professional help or support is necessary:

1. Frequency and Quantity:

- Do I use drugs or alcohol more often than I initially intended?
- Do I consume larger amounts of drugs or alcohol than I used to in order to achieve the desired effect?

2. Loss of Control:

- Do I find it difficult to cut down on or control my substance use?
- Have I unsuccessfully tried to quit or reduce my use in the past?

3. **Craving and Urges:**

- Do I experience strong cravings or urges to use drugs or alcohol?
- Do I feel compelled to use substances in specific situations or to cope with certain emotions?

4. **Neglecting Responsibilities:**

- Have my substance use habits caused me to neglect important work, school, or family responsibilities?
- Am I missing deadlines or failing to meet obligations due to drug or alcohol use?

5. **Interference with Relationships:**

- Have my substance use habits led to conflicts or strained relationships with family, friends, or colleagues?
- Are people close to me expressing concern about my drug or alcohol use?

6. **Social Isolation:**

- Am I withdrawing from social activities and spending more time using substances?
- Do I prioritize substance use over spending time with loved ones?

7. **Risk-Taking Behavior:**

- Have I engaged in risky or dangerous activities while under the influence of drugs or alcohol?
- Do I continue to use substances despite knowing the associated risks?

8. Physical and Psychological Health:

- Have I experienced physical or mental health issues related to my substance use?
- Is my substance use causing me anxiety, depression, or other emotional problems?

9. Tolerance and Withdrawal:

- Have I developed a tolerance, requiring more of the substance to achieve the desired effect?
- Do I experience withdrawal symptoms when I try to cut back or quit?

10. Loss of Interest:

- Have I lost interest in activities I once enjoyed because of my substance use?
- Am I neglecting hobbies, goals, or personal interests because of drugs or alcohol?

11. Financial Impact:

- Have my spending habits been affected by the cost of acquiring drugs or alcohol?
- Am I facing financial difficulties due to my substance use?

12. Legal Issues:

- Have I been involved in legal problems, such as arrests or convictions, related to drug or alcohol use?
- Are legal consequences a result of my substance use?

13. **Denial and Rationalization:**

- Have I minimized or rationalized the negative consequences of my substance use?
- Do I deny or downplay the impact it has on my life?

14. **Failed Attempts to Quit:**

- Have I made multiple unsuccessful attempts to quit or cut back on my substance use?
- Do I find myself returning to substance use shortly after trying to quit?

Answer these questions honestly and without judgment. These are *your* answers, and it's a self-reflection. These questions are for *you*.

If you find that you answer "yes" to several of these questions, or if you have concerns about your substance use, it may be an indication that you have a potential problem worth discussing with your doctor, addiction specialists, counselors, or support groups that can provide guidance and assistance in addressing these issues and working toward recovery. Remember that seeking help is a sign of strength and a crucial step in regaining control of your life. You're reading this book, you're wanting to live a fuller, more intentional life. Removing what gets in your way, including a reliance on drugs or alcohol to get through your day, is possible. The first step is acknowledgement— and recognizing you're worth the effort to make a change.

> Remember that seeking help is a sign of strength and a crucial step in regaining control of your life.

Stop and Reflect

1. Acknowledge your responses to the questions posed above.
2. Write down your responses in your journal and determine what changes, if any, you want or need to implement to keep alcohol/drugs from getting in your way.
3. Put a plan in place.
4. Regularly come back to these plans that you make and assess the level of priority that you want to make this change in your life. Are you taking the steps that you need to in order for you to live your life fully?
5. Are there small habits that you have (like my "Hey! Want to meet for a drink next week?") that you could make a small tweak to? Write down what comes to mind.
6. *Try* it.

Commit to Your Hard Stops

We covered a lot in this section. A lot of things that are on our schedules, on our plates, on our minds, in our lives, can be in the way of us living our best, intentional lives.

Recognize which in the chapter resonated the most with you and take some time to reflect on those. Go to my website and download the "Hard Stop Do Not Do List." Reflect on how you experience each of these in your life and set goals around the small steps you'll take to make big changes. Regularly reviewing and updating this list can help you stay on track and make positive changes in your life.

Now that you know what can get in your way of living a more intentional, content life, we'll discuss how to communicate your priorities and your boundaries to those people in your life important to you so you can get on, and then stay on, your path.

Chapter 12

Communicating Your Priorities

"The way we communicate with others and with ourselves ultimately determines the quality of our lives."

– Tony Robbins

After a lengthy stint at a good company with a great culture and a boss she had an excellent relationship with, Candice was impacted by the most recent round of layoffs. She found herself interviewing for positions for the first time in over a decade. She had years of experience and a solid track record in the industry, and she was quickly hired by a reputable company as a director of product marketing, reporting to the senior vice president.

At the interview, he talked to her about the company's vision, mission, and core values. He talked about how the team "worked hard" and "played hard." They have aggressive goals and require a lot from their team, but it was nothing Candice hadn't dealt with before. She wasn't worried about that. However, once she started, she quickly realized that "work hard" didn't mean just delivering her work on time, within budget, and in a high quality form. To her boss, it meant being willing to work nights and weekends regularly. He operated on a different schedule and expected her (and the rest of the team) to be available when he was. He had access to her calendar to schedule meetings and, consistently, he would schedule them before 8AM, or at 5:30 PM or later—whenever his schedule was open. While in the interview process, he said that travel wasn't a required part of the position; he regularly scheduled team meetings outside "traditional" work hours that added up to a lot of extra nights.

Soon, Candice found herself in a tough position. She used to be able to drop her kids at school and then go into work, but the early morning meetings were now consistently on her calendar. She used to take an exercise class a couple of nights a week after work, but she was having a hard time committing to that because of the team meetings outside standard hours. While still feeling the excitement of a new job, she was also starting to feel that her boss' expectations of her constant availability were causing personal stress and strain in her relationship.

She didn't want to lose her job, but didn't know how to communicate with her boss about priorities that she had outside of work.

Does she need to talk about how important it is for her to drop off kids in the morning and that she can start work at 9:00 AM during the interview process? Or should she wait until she gets offered the job, because the request may come across as her not being as committed as other candidates (and she really needs the job)? Or, should she start working, show she's an outstanding employee, and only then, when they don't want to lose her, is it "safe" for her to communicate her priorities outside of work?

It's a tough call, and there's no one right answer.

In the intricate web of responsibilities and commitments, finding equilibrium in work, relationships, and personal needs not only feels like, but very much can be, a high-stakes juggling act. Articulating priorities requires a delicate balance of assertiveness, empathy, and effective communication. How do you do that? How do you set the stage? And *when* do you have these conversations? This chapter delves into the nuances of engaging in conversations with your manager, your team, and your spouse

> Articulating priorities requires a delicate balance of assertiveness, empathy, and effective communication.

(or significant others) about your priorities, and helps set the stage for conversation about establishing boundaries to help you hit them.

There's no blueprint for these conversations that will ensure you get the outcome that you want, because not all people will react the same. "People will be people," as they say. Some people are more open communicators, some are more empathetic about your life outside of work, some will be more willing to accommodate than others are. There are some bosses who, honestly, won't care what your priorities are outside of your work hours and have expectations like Candice's boss, expecting you to be available when *they* want you to be. I know bosses like that. I've met a lot of them. I know that I, personally, can't work for them, but they're out there. They exist. You may report to one right now. Do you have a direct conversation with them about your priorities?

That's a decision only you can make, but my two cents is this. Personally, I'd rather know. I would rather know who I am working with, how they view me (more transactionally, in what I can do for them in my job, or whether they see me as a whole person with other wishes, desires, and priorities outside of my job), and I want to be able to make decisions based on honest conversations, knowing exactly where we stand.

Our priorities, though, don't just need to be discussed with our managers. Some of our priorities impact the rest of the team we have at work, our partners, and our family.

We'll start with three people/groups of people typically impacted by priorities outside of work: your boss, your team, and your partner.

Communicating with Your Manager

Initiating a conversation with your manager about boundaries necessitates clarity, professionalism, and planning. This is not a conversation where you want to wing it. You need to know in advance what you want to say, what your "ask" is, and be prepared to "sell" why your priorities should matter to *them*. What impact does it have on the business? It is a job, after all.

- Request a time to meet with them; get the time on both of your calendars.
- Start by saying that you want to discuss a topic that's uncomfortable for you to talk about (if it is for you), and ask them if they're open to having that conversation at this time. If not, ask them when a good time would be to have it.

- Acknowledge the significance of your role and what you enjoy about it, how your role helps the company hit their objectives, what you believe you are doing well and that supports the company, as well as where you want to grow with the company, if that's your intention. You are going to talk to them about boundaries, and you want to emphasize that you recognize your position in the company, the importance of it, your *commitment* to it, and that what you are going to discuss next doesn't impact that level of commitment.
- Give background as needed on what you are asking for, and then deliver the ask.
- Depending on the level of your "ask," you may need to propose alternative solutions so that the company can continue to hit the goals they have while accommodating for you.
- Emphasize the benefits of your approach. How does this benefit the company? How does it benefit the team?
- Give them time to consider your ask. Instead of expecting an answer at the end of the conversation, explain that you simply wanted to get a conversation started, you don't expect an answer right away, but you want to have an open dialogue and appreciate their willingness to hear you out.
- Determine next steps. When should you follow up? What questions do they have? Is there anyone else who should be a part of this conversation?

As your priorities will vary drastically, let me give a specific example of this conversation.

A senior level leader in a research company, Alicia, has a mother with dementia. For some time, she was able to take off as emergencies arose or to take her on errands as needed, to be there when her mom would call, but she found that the constant disruptions to her day were having an impact on her being able to concentrate effectively at work. She approached her boss and said that she needed to start work four hours later on Fridays because there were some things that could only be done during traditional work hours when offices are open during the week.

She approached the conversation recognizing that this was a big "ask." She has a big job in the company, she has a team that reports to her, she has client deliverables. All true, but she has other priorities as well. She is an only child and solely responsible for taking care of her mother, so in order to manage both priorities, she would have to be creative to find a way to make it work. She said that by scheduling all of those appointments at one time, her week will be more organized. She can make better plans, instead of having to take off here and there to help, and she can be proactive instead of just reacting to emergencies as they arise.

The manager immediately saw the value in this approach (even if it wasn't standard for a senior leader to be out for four hours a week), but the employee said she would make up the time other days during the week, she would continue to meet company expectations of all clients having a response within twenty-four hours, she would ensure she was on by noon on Fridays to support the team as needed. By all accounts, the arrangement is extremely successful. The employee gets the time she needs to take care of her personal priorities, she is more focused during the other times at work, knowing that she has four hours a week allocated to those other priorities, and she feels respected and appreciated by her employer, making the likelihood that she stays in her position stronger.

I spoke with Melissa Janis, a thirty-year expert in learning and development who also has deep experience as an employment mediator, to get additional suggestions for how to approach these types of conversations. Below, I share the excellent advice she gave me about engaging in these conversations:

- Determine whether you're speaking about a proactive or reactive situation. Has something changed, and you need to react to it (new manager, different expectations, changes to group dynamics?), or are you preparing to get out ahead with your priorities (for example, you're interviewing for a new position)?
- If you're being proactive—considering a new company, a new team, or joining the company—you can start by asking more general questions about expectations. How do they evaluate your effectiveness in your position? Do they talk more about the hours you'll work or the performance you'll deliver? What's it like working for them? What are the team dynamics? What are the company's core values, and how are those represented by their team? You can find out a lot in the proactive stage by asking open-ended questions. These questions should start early—in the interview stage, if possible.

- If you are being more reactive—like Candice, who felt that she joined a team where the boss has unrealistic expectations of how available she should be—Melissa advises not to jump to conclusions about their intentions. For example, she has found that, many times, managers who email or text their teams at nights and on the weekends don't always expect a response back immediately; they simply want to get a task out of their head and off their plate. So, they'll send it without the expectation that their employees will get right back to them. Ask "what is your expectation on turn-around time when you send me messages? Does your turnaround time expectation change if you send a message in the evenings or on the weekends?" Simply start by asking about expectations before assuming there is a bigger conversation to be had. If Candice sees that her boss is typically setting up meetings earlier in the morning than she is typically on, instead of going straight to a "boundaries" conversation, be curious. Ask, "What is your expectation of the time we are available for meetings?" It's very possible a manager is simply finding a time that works in their schedule and hasn't considered that there should be a specific range of times when the team needs to be available. It just may need to be made more explicit.

- You likely have had experiences with your boss that give you an indication of how they may approach this conversation. Some bosses are flexible and some are not. These are different circumstances, and how you approach the conversation will have to vary accordingly. A typical inflexible manager may need to first hear you say that what you're asking for is outside of the standard approach, you know this, and you're asking because... (see steps above where you set the stage, explain the business reason, and then deliver your "ask").

- Melissa likes to ask people entering these types of conversations "what do you really *need*, versus all the things you may want." If you would like to have flexibility in how you set up your day, and to be able to work from home a few days a week, but what you *need* is at least the flexibility to come in at 9:00 after doing a drop-off in the morning, know the difference between need and want. And be willing to pull back to what you need when discussing possible arrangements. That can allow you to reach the best alternative to a negotiated agreement (BATNA, for short)—what you *need* versus what you'd ideally *want*.

- Recognize that your direct manager *may* not be the only person who would need to weigh in on the decision. As you make your case for what you need, think about the impact not only to your boss, but your boss's boss, your team, and the company as a whole. Why does providing you with the flexibility you need (if that's one of your priorities) help the company? How will this enable you to be more productive and deliver better outcomes? With up to 59% of American workers saying they've experienced burnout in their jobs, which translates into higher turnover, show how supporting employees when they need it can have a positive impact on the business.

Having a discussion with your manager about your priorities outside of work isn't an easy conversation for everyone to have, but by planning ahead, anticipating reactions, being direct and professional, and providing potential solutions, you may be surprised. At any rate, you will have answers, instead of questioning whether it's possible.

Communicating with Your Team

Honest discussions about individual priorities foster mutual understanding and cohesion, and, in my experience, help build the team culture. But some people on the team will be less supportive than others. Using the same example above, people in the company may see someone not working on Fridays until noon and want to know why they are getting special treatment. They may say it's unfair that they have to pick up the slack when the other person isn't there. They may want to know what's in it for them.

But, people are also *people*. Not just workers. Not just people on the team. People who can understand what other people are going through, if given the opportunity to have that direct conversation. In my experience, when people are open and honest with each other about what's going on in their lives, more often than not, there's empathy, understanding, and a willingness to help.

The senior leader, Alicia, who needed to take off every Friday? At the company's weekly meeting, the CEO set the stage by talking about the company's core values. About how the company was built around delivering exceptional results while creating a culture that allows people to have balance in their lives. The CEO further explained that they have built a team that supports each other, constantly stepping in for each other when someone's workload is far greater than their own. She gave multiple examples of how the team has stepped in when others needed it.

After this opening, she asked Alicia to speak to the team. Alicia shared the backstory on the situation with her mother, explained how helping her mom is a top priority, as is ensuring that she continued to meet all deadlines and responsibilities of the company. To do the latter as best she could, she worked with the leadership team to take four hours off every Friday for the reasons already outlined above, and she explained how no one else would be expected to fill in for her, she would simply work later and catch up over the weekends if needed. There wasn't a dry eye when she was done speaking; the team just wanted to know how they could help.

Companies may not have to offer the *same* thing to all employees, but may need to offer *some* things at some times that particular employee needs. The key is communication. Open, honest, direct communication wins out in the end, usually.

Stop and Reflect

1. Do any of your priorities impact your team?
2. If so, which ones specifically, and how do they impact your team?

3. Think about how those on your team may *think* your priorities would impact them and write out those potential concerns.

4. Be ready to rebut their concerns, if they are unfounded. Your team will be most concerned about how what you share will impact *them.*

5. Set aside time to meet with your team.

6. Set the stage or have another on your team set the stage if needed (example above).

7. Be direct, honest, and ask if anyone has concerns or questions.

8. Each situation will be different, and some priorities that you have won't require a conversation with your team. Alicia's did. Her team could see she was no longer in the office for four hours on Friday. It would have been noticed. Others may not require this type of communication, but if it is warranted, plan ahead and prepare using the steps above.

Communicating with Your Partner

When you look at your list of priorities, some are going to require buy-in from your partner. If you want to make it to the gym three nights a week and you have kids, your partner will have to step in for you. If you are prioritizing a big promotion at work and you need to work more nights and weekends, you need to be direct with your partner about your goals and your reasoning for extended hours, and ask for the support you need while you're working towards this goal.

When I decided that I wanted to write this book—while working full time at the company I own, mom-ing, being a partner, and still wanting to maintain time for my physical and mental health—I had to have a conversation with my partner about what it would mean for my family, for us, and, specifically, for him.

The only time in the day I was guaranteed uninter-rupted thinking time is in the morning. Early morning. I can start writing at six in the morning and have an hour and a half before I have to wake up the kids to get ready for school. I could prioritize this book, I could create the time for it (I did both of these things), but it meant that I needed *him* to understand that I couldn't be up late watching mov-ies with him at night. I had to move up my time to sleep to 9:30, which meant we needed to move up the time we ate dinner; everything just had to shift a bit to accommodate me. It was a change. And that change was needed to get me to this point, where this (close to) final chapter is being written. I needed his buy-in to do so.

Partnerships are unique, so you'll know best how to communicate with your partner to get the buy-in needed for your priorities. I've found that communicating your goals and aspirations to align expectations is a great start. I follow this type of format (not verbatim):

"Here's the big picture. Here's why I want to do what I want to do. This is why it's important to me. I know that it will come with some changes to how we operate now, and will require some compromise and support, and I want to make sure that this is something that you can support me on (ask for support directly). It's really import-ant to me and I'd appreciate your support. We'll see how these changes work, and we'll just need to be open and honest with each other about what's working and what's not so we can adjust as needed. Does that work for you? Is this something you can support me on?"

I just ask, directly, if I'll get the support on big changes. Then there's no animosity. I can come back to the direct conversation and say, "We talked about this. I asked for your support. I said this is why it was so important to me. Did anything change?" and we more quickly get back on track.

Navigating conversations about priorities with various stakeholders involves a delicate interplay of assertiveness, empathy, and adaptability. These conversations aren't always easy, and there's no magic blueprint that will work for each one of these. The most important thing is that you have the conversations. You are open, you're honest. Only then can others understand your perspective and support you (or not), and then you know and can adjust as needed.

Conclusion

We're doing something new with this final section by *starting* with the **self-reflection** questions.

Stop and Reflect

1. Think back to when you first picked up this book. Grab your journal and take time to revisit the journey that you've just been on.
2. What made you decide to read a book about intentionality?
3. What were you hoping to get out of reading *Hard Stop?*
4. What did you discover about yourself along the way?
5. What did you start doing that you want to continue doing on this path?
6. What have you committed to not doing that will help you on this path?
7. How has defining your priorities impacted you?

8. In what ways did defining specific, measurable, attainable, relatable, and timely goals impact you professionally and/or personally?
9. Are you leaving with your core values defined and your personal mission statement?
10. What *hard stops* did you realize you need to confront?
11. How are you holding yourself accountable to do so?

You started a journey by reading *Hard Stop.*

You may have started this journey because you were feeling like you were on a hamster wheel: always moving, always busy, but going nowhere. You may have felt directionless. Going through the motions without goals in place, without priorities identified explicitly and not always getting your time. You may have felt that everyone else's priorities were getting the best of you and you were getting the scraps left over at the end of the day. You may have lamented the fact that there was no time in your day. You may have picked up this book as it was recommended to you, or you were simply supporting me and one of my dreams of becoming an author—thank you, if that's the case!—but never gave time to consider these questions before.

However, and for whatever reasons you started reading this book, if you're reading this sentence, **you have made yourself a priority.** You've made your *priorities* a priority. If you've done the activities, I hope you are leaving with a better sense of where you want to go, and most importantly, *why*, and have given yourself goals that you can hold yourself accountable to in order to live the life you want to live.

I wrote this book because I am fiercely passionate about living life. **Now**. Not when I have more money, not when I get the next promotion, not when I retire, not when I get sick and realize there's more to life, not later—**now**. I want you to find ways to create time in your life to do what a friend of mine says "sets her soul on fire."

I want you to be able to create a life that's rich in *all* areas that are important to you.

I applaud you for taking this step, for making time for *you*, and for getting clear on the life you want to live.

As I always say, the most important step in practicing intentionality is **starting**.

The next most important step is **continuing**.

As I've said throughout the book, the self-reflection exercises you do can feel uncomfortable. Goals may

> I want you to be able to create a life that's rich in *all* areas that are important to you.

feel clunky at first, but, trust me, they get easier over time! Being so meticulous about how you spend your time will feel awkward. And tedious. And annoying—at first. But the more you do it, the easier and more natural it becomes. And the more you do it, the less time you allow yourself to aimlessly drift, unsure of where you want to go.

Your intentionality practice doesn't have to be perfect. It simply needs to exist.

I urge you to continue what you started in these pages. Find five to ten minutes in your day to check in with yourself. It doesn't have to be more than that. This is sustainable! Write in your journal. Plan your day. Plan your week. Plan your month. Plan your life. And then, don't stop.

Use the resources available online and follow the *Hard Stop* blog at www.ginaboedeker.com to continue finding inspiration, as well as practical tips, to help you live intentionally every day.

Thanks for allowing me to be a part of your journey.

Review Inquiry

Hey, it's Gina here.

I hope you've enjoyed the book, finding it both useful and fun. I have a favor to ask you.

Would you consider giving it a rating wherever you bought the book? Online book stores are more likely to promote a book when they feel good about its content, and reader reviews are a great barometer for a book's quality.

Please go to the website of wherever you bought the book, search for my name and the book title, and leave a review. If able, perhaps consider adding a picture of you holding the book. That increases the likelihood your review will be accepted! Plus I'll know you're on your intentionality journey and that means a lot to me!

Many thanks in advance,

Gina Boedeker

Will You Share the Love?

Get this book for a friend, associate, or family member!

If you have found this book valuable and know others who would find it useful, consider buying them a copy as a gift. Special bulk discounts are available if you would like your whole team or organization to benefit from reading this. Just contact me through the website www.ginaboedeker.com.

Would You Like Gina Boedeker to Speak to Your Organization?

Book Gina Now!

Gina Boedeker accepts a limited number of speaking engagements each year. To learn how you can bring her message to your organization, contact her directly through the website at www.ginaboedeker.com.

About the Author

 Gina Boedeker is the founder and CEO of The Boedeker Group (TBG), a market research company that helps their clients gather insights from their target markets to help grow their businesses. After fifteen years in publishing, she left her role as managing director of a global educational publisher to start her own company—one that offered the flexibility she needed to "mom" on her own terms and pursue passions outside of work.

She believes fiercely that you can deliver exceptional results professionally *while* living a full life. Making time for your passions, hobbies, adventures, friends, family and other priorities *should* be what you create your time around. She built her company around this premise and has grown it from an idea stage to a seven-figure business without having to sacrifice what is most important to her in her life.

That's the message she wants to share and is her motivation for writing *Hard Stop*. She wants more people to live their lives with intention and without regret.

Originally from St. Louis, MO, she lived in New York City for fifteen years before moving to Boulder, Colorado with her family in 2020. She has a husband (Otavio), a daughter (Elena), and a son (Luiz). They are loving their lives out west and enjoy everything the mountains have to offer: climbing, hiking, skiing, ice climbing, even uphill skiing—yes! That's a thing!

Gina can be reached at www.ginaboedeker.com.

Made in the USA
Middletown, DE
05 September 2024

60434702R00139